PATHWAYS

Listening, Speaking, and Critical Thinking

1A

Becky Tarver Chase

NATIONAL GEOGRAPHIC LEARNING | CENGAGE Learning®

Andover • Melbourne • Mexico City • Stamford, CT • Toronto • Hong Kong • New Delhi • Seoul • Singapore • Tokyo

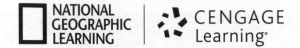

Pathways Split Text 1A
Listening, Speaking, and Critical Thinking
Becky Tarver Chase

Regional Director, Asia ELT/School:
Michael Cahill

Publisher, Asia ELT/School: Edward Yoshioka

Production Manager (Asia): Pauline Lim

Production Executive (Asia): Cindy Chai

Publisher: Sherrise Roehr

Executive Editor: Laura Le Dréan

Acquisitions Editor: Tom Jefferies

Senior Development Editor: Mary Whittemore

Development Editor: Paul Carne

Director of Global Marketing: Ian Martin

Marketing Manager: Caitlin Thomas

Marketing Manager: Katie Kelley

Marketing Manager: Emily Stewart

Director of Content and Media Production:
Michael Burggren

Content Project Manager: Daisy Sosa

Manufacturing Manager: Marcia Locke

Manufacturing Buyer: Marybeth Hennebury

Cover Design: Page 2 LLC

Cover Image: RAUL TOUZON/National
Geographic Image Collection

Interior Design: Page 2 LLC

Composition: Cenveo Publisher Services/
Nesbitt Graphics, Inc.

For product information and technology assistance, contact us at
Cengage Learning Asia Customer Support, 65-6410-1200

For permission to use material from this text or product,
submit all requests online at **www.cengageasia.com/permissions**
Further permissions questions can be emailed to
asia.permissionrequest@cengage.com

ISBN 13: 978-1-285-15969-0
ISBN 10: 1-285-15969-1

Cengage Learning Asia Pte Ltd
151 Lorong Chuan #02-08
New Tech Park
Singapore 556741

National Geographic Learning
20 Channel Center St.
Boston, MA 02210
USA

Cengage Learning is a leading provider of customized learning solutions with office locations around the globe, including Andover, Melbourne, Mexico City, Stamford (CT), Toronto, Hong Kong, New Delhi, Seoul, Singapore, and Tokyo. Locate your local office at **www.cengage.com/global**

Cengage Learning products are represented in Canada by Nelson Education, Ltd.

Visit National Geographic Learning online at **ngl.cengage.com**
For product information, visit our website at **www.cengageasia.com**

Printed in Singapore
2 3 4 5 6 7 8 16 15 14 13

ACKNOWLEDGEMENTS

The author and publisher would like to thank the following reviewers:

UNITED STATES Adrianne Aiko Thompson, Miami Dade College, Miami, Florida; **Gokhan Alkanat**, Auburn University at Montgomery, Alabama; **Nikki Ashcraft**, Shenandoah University, VA; **Karin Avila-John**, University of Dayton, Ohio; **Shirley Baker**, Alliant International University, California; **John Baker**, Oakland Community College, Michigan; **Evina Baquiran Torres**, Zoni Language Centers, New York; **Michelle Bell**, University of South Florida, Florida; **Nancy Boyer**, Golden West College, California; **Carol Brutza**, Gateway Community College, Connecticut; **Sarah Camp**, University of Kentucky, Center for ESL, Kentucky; **Maria Caratini**, Eastfield College, Texas; **Ana Maria Cepero**, Miami Dade College, Miami, Florida; **Daniel Chaboya**, Tulsa Community College, Oklahoma; **Patricia Chukwueke**, English Language Institute – UCSD Extension, California; **Julia A. Correia**, Henderson State University, Connecticut; **Suzanne Crisci**, Bunker Hill Community College, Massachusetts; **Katie Crowder**, University of North Texas, Texas; **Lynda Dalgish**, Concordia College, New York; **Jeffrey Diluglio**, Center for English Language and Orientation Programs: Boston University, Massachusetts; **Tim DiMatteo**, Southern New Hampshire University, New Hampshire; **Scott Dirks**, Kaplan International Center at Harvard Square, Massachusetts; **Margo Downey**, Center for English Language and Orientation Programs: Boston University, Massachusetts; **John Drezek**, Richland College, Texas; **Anwar El-Issa**, Antelope Valley College, California; **Anrisa Fannin**, The International Education Center at Diablo Valley College, California; **Jennie Farnell**, University of Connecticut, American Language Program, Connecticut; **Mark Fisher**, Lone Star College, Texas; **Celeste Flowers**, University of Central Arkansas, Arkansas; **John Fox**, English Language Institute, Georgia; **Pradel R. Frank**, Miami Dade College, Florida; **Sally Gearheart**, Santa Rosa Jr. College, California; **Karen Grubbs**, ELS Language Centers, Florida; **Joni Hagigeorges**, Salem State University, Massachusetts; **Valerie Heming**, University of Central Missouri, Missouri; **Mary Hill**, North Shore Community College, Massachusetts; **Harry L. Holden**, North Lake College, Texas; **Ingrid Holm**, University of Massachusetts Amherst, Massachusetts; **Marianne Hsu Santelli**, Middlesex County College, New Jersey; **Katie Hurter**, Lone Star College – North Harris, Texas; **Justin Jernigan**, Georgia Gwinnett College, Georgia; **Barbara A. Jonckheere**, American Language Institute at California State University, Long Beach, California; **Susan Jordan**, Fisher College, Massachusetts; **Maria Kasparova**, Bergen Community College, New Jersey; **Gail Kellersberger**, University of Houston-Downtown, Texas; **Christina Kelso**, Austin Peay State University, Tennessee; **Daryl Kinney**, Los Angeles City College, California; **Leslie Kosel Eckstein**, Hillsborough Community College, Florida; **Beth Kozbial Ernst**, University of Wisconsin-Eau Claire, Wisconsin; **Jennifer Lacroix**, Center for English Language and Orientation Programs: Boston University, Massachusetts; **Stuart Landers**, Missouri State University, Missouri; **Margaret V. Layton**, University of Nevada, Reno Intensive English Language Center, Nevada; **Heidi Lieb**, Bergen Community College, New Jersey; **Kerry Linder**, Language Studies International New York, New York; **Jenifer Lucas-Uygun**, Passaic County Community College, New Jersey; **Alison MacAdams**, Approach International Student Center, Massachusetts; **Craig Machado**, Norwalk Community College, Connecticut; **Andrew J. MacNeill**, Southwestern College, California; **Melanie A. Majeski**, Naugatuck Valley Community College, Connecticut; **Wendy Maloney**, College of DuPage, Illinois; **Chris Mares**, University of Maine – Intensive English Institute, Maine; **Josefina Mark**, Union County College, New Jersey; **Connie Mathews**, Nashville State Community College, Tennessee; **Bette Matthews**, Mid-Pacific Institute, Hawaii; **Marla McDaniels Heath**, Norwalk Community College, Connecticut; **Kimberly McGrath Moreira**, University of Miami, Florida; **Sara McKinnon**, College of Marin, California; **Christine Mekkaoui**, Pittsburg State University, Kansas; **Holly A. Milkowart**, Johnson County Community College, Kansas; **Warren Mosher**, University of Miami, Florida; **Lukas Murphy**, Westchester Community College, New York; **Elena Nehrebecki**, Hudson Community College, New Jersey; **Bjarne Nielsen**, Central Piedmont Community College, North Carolina; **David Nippoldt**, Reedley College, California; **Lucia Parsley**, Virginia Commonwealth University, Virginia; **Wendy Patriquin**, Parkland College, Illinois; **Marion Piccolomini**, Communicate With Ease, LTD, Pennsylvania; **Carolyn Prager**, Spanish-American Institute, New York; **Eileen Prince**, Prince Language Associates Incorporated, Massachusetts; **Sema Pulak**, Texas A & M University, Texas; **James T. Raby**, Clark University, Massachusetts; **Anouchka Rachelson**, Miami-Dade College, Florida; **Lynn Ramage Schaefer**, University of Central Arkansas, Arkansas; **Sherry Rasmussen**, DePaul University, Illinois; **Amy Renehan**, University of Washington, Washington; **Esther Robbins**, Prince George's Community College, Pennsylvania; **Helen Roland**, Miami Dade College, Florida; **Linda Roth**, Vanderbilt University English Language Center, Tennessee; **Janine Rudnick**, El Paso Community College, Texas; **Rita Rutkowski Weber**, University of Wisconsin – Milwaukee, Wisconsin; **Elena Sapp**, INTO Oregon State University, Oregon; **Margaret Shippey**, Miami Dade College, Florida; **Lisa Sieg**, Murray State University, Kentucky; **Alison Stamps**, ESL Center at Mississippi State University, Mississippi; **Peggy Street**, ELS Language Centers, Miami, Florida; **Lydia Streiter**, York College Adult Learning Center, New York; **Nicholas Taggart**, Arkansas State University, Arkansas; **Marcia Takacs**, Coastline Community College, California; **Tamara Teffeteller**, University of California Los Angeles, American Language Center, California; **Rebecca Toner**, English Language Programs, University of Pennsylvania, Pennsylvania; **William G. Trudeau**, Missouri Southern State University, Missouri; **Troy Tucker**, Edison State College, Florida; **Maria Vargas-O'Neel**, Miami Dade College, Florida; **Amerca Vazquez**, Miami Dade College, Florida; **Alison Vinande**, Modesto Junior College, California; **Christie Ward**, Intensive English Language Program, Central Connecticut State University, Connecticut; **Colin S. Ward**, Lone Star College-North Harris, Texas; **Denise L. Warner**, Lansing Community College, Michigan; **Wendy Wish-Bogue**, Valencia Community College, Florida; **Cissy Wong**, Sacramento City College, California; **Kimberly Yoder**, Kent State University, ESL Center, Ohio.

ASIA Teoh Swee Ai, Universiti Teknologi Mara, Malaysia; **Nor Azni Abdullah**, Universiti Teknologi Mara, Malaysia; **Thomas E. Bieri**, Nagoya College, Japan;

Paul Bournhonesque, Seoul National University of Technology, Korea; **Michael C. Cheng**, National Chengchi University, Taiwan; **Fu-Dong Chiou**, National Taiwan University, Taiwan; **Derek Currie**, Korea University, Sejong Institute of Foreign Language Studies, Korea; **Christoph A. Hafner**, City University of Hong Kong, Hong Kong; **Wenhua Hsu**, I-Shou University, Taiwan; **Helen Huntley**, Hanoi University, Vietnam; **Rob Higgens**, Ritsumeikan University, Japan; **Shih Fan Kao**, JinWen University of Science and Technology, Taiwan; **Ikuko Kashiwabara**, Osaka Electro-Communication University, Japan; **Richard S. Lavin**, Prefecturla University of Kumamoto, Japan;

Mike Lay, American Institute, Cambodia; **Byoung-Kyo Lee**, Yonsei University, Korea; **Lin Li**, Capital Normal University, China; **Hudson Murrell**, Baiko Gakuin University, Japan; **Keiichi Narita**, Niigata University, Japan; **Huynh Thi Ai Nguyen**, Vietnam USA Society, Vietnam; **James Pham**, IDP Phnom Penh, Cambodia; **Duncan Rose**, British Council, Singapore; **Simone Samuels**, The Indonesia Australia Language Foundation Jakarta, Indonesia; **Wang Songmei**, Beijing Institute of Education Faculty, China; **Chien-Wen Jenny Tseng**, National Sun Yat-Sen University, Taiwan; **Hajime Uematsu**, Hirosaki University, Japan **AUSTRALIA Susan Austin**, University of South Australia, **Joanne Cummins**, Swinburne College; **Pamela Humphreys**, Griffith University **LATIN AMERICA AND THE CARIBBEAN Ramon Aguilar**, Universidad Tecnológica de Hermosillo, México; **Livia de Araujo Donnini Rodrigues**, University of São Paolo, Brazil; **Cecilia Avila**, Universidad de Xapala, México; **Beth Bartlett**, Centro Cultural Colombo Americano, Cali, Colombia; **Raúl Billini**, Colegio Loyola, Dominican Republic; **Nohora Edith Bryan**, Universidad de La Sabana, Colombia;

Raquel Hernández Cantú, Instituto Tecnológico de Monterrey, Mexico; **Millie Commander**, Inter American University of Puerto Rico, Puerto Rico; **Edwin Marin-Arroyo**, Instituto Tecnológico de Costa Rica; **Rosario Mena**, Instituto Cultural Dominico-Americano, Dominican Republic; **Elizabeth Ortiz Lozada**, COPEI-COPOL English Institute, Ecuador; **Gilberto Rios Zamora**, Sinaloa State Language Center, Mexico; **Patricia Veciños**, El Instituto Cultural Argentino Norteamericano, Argentina **MIDDLE EAST AND NORTH AFRICA Tom Farkas**, American University of Cairo, Egypt; **Ghada Hozayen**, Arab Academy for Science, Technology and Maritime Transport, Egypt; **Jodi Lefort**, Sultan Qaboos University, Muscat, Oman; **Barbara R. Reimer**, CERTESL, UAE University, UAE

Scope and Sequence

Grammar	Speaking Skills	Viewing	Critical Thinking Skills
The simple present tense vs. the present continuous Adverbs of frequency	Communicating that you don't understand Doing a career-aptitude interview Using adverbs of frequency to discuss a work schedule **Student to Student:** Giving feedback while listening **Presentation Skills:** Introducing yourself	Video: *Butler School* Activating prior knowledge Viewing for general understanding Relating the video to career choices	Making inferences Evaluating career options Explaining a job's impact on the world Reflecting on the content of an interview Using a chart to organize notes for a presentation **Critical Thinking Focus:** Identifying main ideas
The simple present tense: *Yes/No* questions The simple present tense: *Wh-* questions Recognizing past tense signal words	Asking questions to show interest Making small talk **Student to Student:** Asking for repetition **Presentation Skills:** Speaking to a group	Video: *Nubian Wedding* Using a map to learn background information Viewing for specific information Discussing the video in the context of one's own experience	Identifying what makes us laugh Judging the appropriateness of laughter Considering benefits and drawbacks Ranking the importance of benefits Generating questions about a presentation **Critical Thinking Focus:** Understanding the speaker's purpose
The simple past tense *Yes/No* questions in the simple past tense *Wh-* questions in the simple past tense	Expressing agreement informally Asking questions about past events **Student to Student:** Making informal suggestions **Presentation Skills:** Speaking from notes	Video: *Treasures in Old San Juan* Viewing to confirm predictions Note-taking while viewing Understanding sound bites from the video	Recognizing the value of the past Understanding information on a timeline Recalling information about a classmate Ranking ways to improve one's memory Evaluating one's own methods for remembering information **Critical Thinking Focus:** Recalling facts
Count and noncount nouns *A/n*, *any*, and *some*	Expressing likes and dislikes Expressing quantity with noncount nouns Comparing quantities or amounts **Student to Student:** Showing thanks and appreciation **Presentation Skills:** Making eye contact	Video: *Tornado Chase* Using a dictionary Viewing for specific information Discussing the video in the context of the unit theme	Reflecting on ideas about the weather Using prior knowledge in a group discussion Choosing appropriate activities for different types of weather Categorizing information from a map Discussing climate change **Critical Thinking Focus:** Making a list
Can and *can't* Descriptive adjectives	Expressing opinions Conducting a survey about eating habits Describing a favorite food **Student to Student:** Showing agreement **Presentation Skills:** Giving interesting details	Video: *Forbidden Fruit* Viewing for general understanding Understanding vocabulary from the video Expressing opinions	Discussing food and culture Selecting interesting information from survey results Categorizing new vocabulary Ranking important aspects of a restaurant or cafeteria Assessing a conversation **Critical Thinking Focus:** Distinguishing between main ideas and details

Each unit consists of two lessons which include the following sections:

- Building Vocabulary
- Using Vocabulary
- Developing Listening Skills
- Exploring Spoken English
- Speaking (called "Engage" in Lesson B)

An **academic pathway** is clearly labeled for learners, starting with formal listening (e.g., lectures) and moving to a more informal context (e.g., a conversation between students in a study group).

The **"Exploring the Theme"** section provides a visual introduction to the unit and encourages learners to think critically and share ideas about the unit topic.

UNIT
9

Our Relationship with Nature

ACADEMIC PATHWAYS
Lesson A: Listening to a Lecture
            Comparing Three Natural Attractions
Lesson B: Listening to a Conversation
            Giving an Individual Presentation

Think and Discuss
1. Look at the photo. What is this man doing?
2. Is this something you might like to do? Explain.
3. What do you think you will learn about in this unit?

Alvaro del Campo feeds hungry macaws, Tambopata National Reserve, Peru.

161

Exploring the Theme:
Our Relationship with Nature

Look at the photos and read the captions. Then discuss the questions.

1. What do you see on these pages that represents the natural world?
2. Which of the photos on these pages show a good relationship between people and nature? Which photos show a bad relationship? Explain.
3. What can people do in order to have a positive effect on the natural world?

Sharing Land with Animals

When people and animals have to share the same land, it sometimes causes conflicts, or problems. This polar bear is looking through a cabin window in Svalbard, Norway.

Hunting and Fishing

These Senegalese fishermen are pulling in nets filled with fish. People fish and hunt animals for food. Fishing is the main reason there are fewer large fish in the oceans today than in the past.

Scientific Research

Biologists are scientists who study living things. The information biologists collect can help the animals they study. This biologist is studying Macaroni penguins on Bird Island, South Georgia.

The top of the volcano Santa Maria appears through the clouds in the western highlands of Guatemala.

162 | UNIT 9

OUR RELATIONSHIP WITH NATURE | 163

Key academic and high-frequency vocabulary
is introduced, practiced, and expanded throughout
each unit. Lessons A and B each present and
practice 10 terms.

A **"Developing Listening Skills"**
section follows a before, during, and after
listening approach to give learners the tools
necessary to master listening skills for a
variety of contexts.

Listening activities
encourage learners to listen for and
consolidate key information, reinforcing
the language, and allowing learners to
think critically about the information they hear.

LESSON A   BUILDING VOCABULARY

A | **Using a Dictionary.** Listen and check (✔) the words you already know. Use a dictionary to help you with any new words. These are words you will hear and use in Lesson A.

☐ ahead (adv.) ☐ hunt (v.) ☐ relationship (n.) ☐ responsibility (n.) ☐ value (v.)
☐ depend (v.) ☐ raise (v.) ☐ respect (n.) ☐ share (v.) ☐ within (prep.)

B | **Meaning from Context.** Read the two articles below. Fill in each blank with a word from the box above it. There is one extra word in each box. Then listen and check your answers.

| ahead | depend | raise | relationship | share |

The Maasai People and Cattle[1]

The Maasai people of East Africa have a special (1) _____ with one kind of animal. They (2) _____ on cattle for meat and milk, which make up most of the Maasai diet. In order to (3) _____ cattle in a dry climate, the Maasai people (4) _____ land. Each family has its own animals, but they move the cattle over long distances and onto different families' land in order to find enough grass for the cattle to eat.

[1]Cattle are the large animals that beef comes from.

| ahead | respect | value | within |

The Sami People and Reindeer

Like the Maasai, the Sami people of northern Europe (5) _____ one animal more than any other. In this difficult climate, reindeer give the Sami people food, clothing, and other useful items. Nowadays, some Sami people raise reindeer on farms, but many Sami people still travel long distances with their animals. This gives them a detailed knowledge of the land and a great (6) _____ for nature. No one knows exactly what is (7) _____ for the Sami people because climate change makes the future of the Arctic uncertain.

164 | UNIT 9

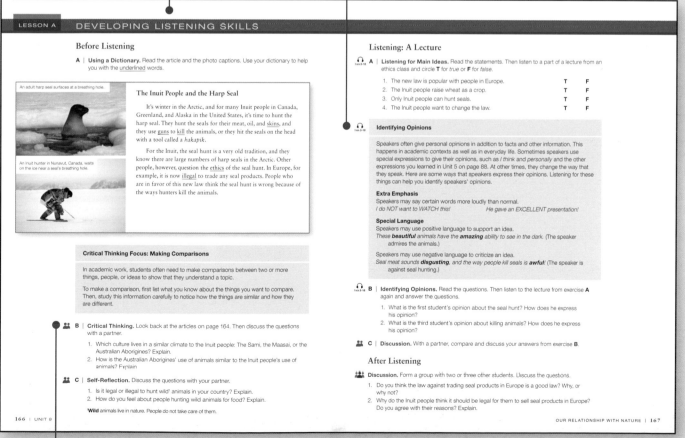

LESSON A   DEVELOPING LISTENING SKILLS

Before Listening

A | **Using a Dictionary.** Read the article and the photo captions. Use your dictionary to help you with the underlined words.

An adult harp seal surfaces at a breathing hole.

An Inuit hunter in Nunavut, Canada, waits on the ice near a seal's breathing hole.

The Inuit People and the Harp Seal

It's winter in the Arctic, and for many Inuit people in Canada, Greenland, and Alaska in the United States, it's time to hunt the harp seal. They hunt the seals for their meat, oil, and skins, and they use guns to kill the animals, or they hit the seals on the head with a tool called a *hakapik*.

For the Inuit, the seal hunt is a very old tradition, and they know there are large numbers of harp seals in the Arctic. Other people, however, question the ethics of the seal hunt. In Europe, for example, it is now illegal to trade any seal products. People who are in favor of this new law think the seal hunt is wrong because of the ways hunters kill the animals.

Critical Thinking Focus: Making Comparisons

In academic work, students often need to make comparisons between two or more things, people, or ideas to show that they understand a topic.

To make a comparison, first list what you know about the things you want to compare. Then, study this information carefully to notice how the things are similar and how they are different.

B | **Critical Thinking.** Look back at the articles on page 164. Then discuss the questions with a partner.
1. Which culture lives in a similar climate to the Inuit people: The Sami, the Maasai, or the Australian Aborigines? Explain.
2. How is the Australian Aborigines' use of animals similar to the Inuit people's use of animals? Explain.

C | **Self-Reflection.** Discuss the questions with your partner.
1. Is it legal or illegal to hunt wild[1] animals in your country? Explain.
2. How do you feel about people hunting wild animals for food? Explain.

[1]Wild animals live in nature. People do not take care of them.

166 | UNIT 9

Listening: A Lecture

A | **Listening for Main Ideas.** Read the statements. Then listen to a part of a lecture from an ethics class and circle **T** for *true* or **F** for *false*.

1. The new law is popular with people in Europe.   T   F
2. The Inuit people raise wheat as a crop.   T   F
3. Only Inuit people can hunt seals.   T   F
4. The Inuit people want to change the law.   T   F

Identifying Opinions

Speakers often give personal opinions in addition to facts and other information. This happens in academic contexts as well as in everyday life. Sometimes speakers use special expressions to give their opinions, such as *I think* and *personally* and the other expressions you learned in Unit 5 on page 88. At other times, they change the way that they speak. Here are some ways that speakers express their opinions. Listening for these things can help you identify speakers' opinions.

Extra Emphasis
Speakers may say certain words more loudly than normal.
I do NOT want to WATCH this!   *He gave an EXCELLENT presentation!*

Special Language
Speakers may use positive language to support an idea.
*These **beautiful** animals have the **amazing** ability to see in the dark.* (The speaker admires the animals.)

Speakers may use negative language to criticize an idea.
*Seal meat sounds **disgusting**, and the way people kill seals is **awful**!* (The speaker is against seal hunting.)

B | **Identifying Opinions.** Read the questions. Then listen to the lecture from exercise **A** again and answer the questions.
1. What is the first student's opinion about the seal hunt? How does he express his opinion?
2. What is the third student's opinion about killing animals? How does he express his opinion?

C | **Discussion.** With a partner, compare and discuss your answers from exercise **B**.

After Listening

Discussion. Form a group with two or three other students. Discuss the questions.
1. Do you think the law against trading seal products in Europe is a good law? Why, or why not?
2. Why do the Inuit people think it should be legal for them to sell seal products in Europe? Do you agree with their reasons? Explain.

OUR RELATIONSHIP WITH NATURE | 167

Critical thinking activities are integrated in every unit, encouraging
continuous engagement in developing academic skills.

LESSON A | EXPLORING SPOKEN ENGLISH

Grammar

The Comparative and Superlative Forms of Adjectives

We use the comparative form to talk about differences between two people or things. With most one-syllable or two-syllable adjectives, we form the comparative with verb + -er (+ than).

> Polar bears are **larger than** black bears. They also live in a **colder** climate.

With adjectives that have more than two syllables, we form the comparative with *more* or *less*.

> Brett is **more responsible than** his brother. He's **less interesting**, though.

We use the superlative to talk about extremes among three or more people or things. With most one or two-syllable adjectives, we form the superlative with *the* + -est.

> Mount Everest is **the highest** mountain in the world.

With adjectives that have more than two syllables, we form the superlative with *the most* or *the least*.

> Miranda is **the most intelligent** child in the class, but she is the least **friendly**.

A | With a partner, take turns saying the sentences below with the comparative or superlative form of the adjective in parentheses.

> Frank is the tallest member of my family.

1. Frank is (tall) member of my family.
2. Fishing is (dangerous) job in my country.
3. Your cookies are (delicious) than my cookies.
4. This view is (beautiful) than the view from my hotel room.
5. Your apartment is (clean) apartment in the building.
6. I think cattle are (smart) than horses.

Spelling Changes and Irregular Forms of the Comparative and Superlative

There are a few extra rules for spelling comparative and superlative adjectives correctly.

- With words ending in e, just add -r or -st: safe-safer large-largest
- With words ending in y, change the y to i: lazy-lazier happy-happiest
- With words ending in consonant-vowel-consonant, double the final consonant:
  hot-hotter thin-thinnest

Some common adjectives have irregular comparative and superlative forms.
> good–better–best bad–worse–worst far–farther–farthest

168 | UNIT 9

B | With a partner, complete each sentence with the comparative or superlative form of the adjective in parentheses. Then practice saying the sentences.

1. My house is ___farther___ (far) from here than your house is.
2. African elephants have _____ (big) ears than Asian elephants have.
3. The monkeys at the zoo are _____ (noisy) than monkeys in the wild.
4. This rose is _____ (pretty) flower in my garden.
5. The _____ (bad) grade I got in any of my classes this semester was a C.
6. My apartment is _____ (small) than your apartment.

Language Function: Making Comparisons

A | Look at the photos and read the captions. Then read and listen to the information about two studies of black bears. Notice the similarities and differences between the two studies.

Black Bear Research: Two Places and Two Methods

North American black bears are shy animals. They are fearful by nature, and will usually run away if they see or hear people. Because of this, it can be difficult for scientists to learn about these animals.

In order to study black bears, researchers in the state of New Jersey, USA, catch bears in traps.[1] Then they sedate the bears with drugs, so they go to sleep and cannot move for a short time. Researchers then measure and weigh the bear, remove a tooth to find out the bear's age, and take blood to test for diseases. From these studies, researchers want to find out how many bears live in New Jersey, how long they live, and how many babies, or cubs, they produce.

Several hundred miles to the west, another black bear study is taking place in Minnesota, USA. There, Dr. Lynn Rogers and his team study bears that are completely awake. The bears know the researchers' voices and they are not afraid of the team. They still run away from other people, but with the help of a few grapes or nuts to keep the bears busy, Dr. Rogers can touch the animals to check their hearts, look at their teeth, and change the radio or GPS[3] equipment that the bears wear around their necks. He and his team can also walk or sit with the bears for hours and make videos to learn about the bears' everyday lives.

In both places, the main goal is the same—to make sure there is a healthy population of wild black bears. In contrast, the research methods and the kinds of information researchers are able to collect are quite different.

A researcher from the New Jersey Department of Environmental Protection measures a sedated black bear.

Dr. Lynn Rogers of the Wildlife[2] Research Institute in Minnesota observes a black bear that is wearing a radio collar.

[1]A **trap** catches and holds an animal that walks into it.
[2]**Wildlife** refers to the animals and other things that live in the wild.
[3]**GPS** (Global Positioning System) equipment allows researchers to follow the bears' movements with satellite technology.

OUR RELATIONSHIP WITH NATURE | 169

• The **"Exploring Spoken English"** section allows students to examine and practice specific grammar points and language functions from the unit while enabling them to sharpen their listening and speaking skills.

• Lesson A closes with a **full page of "Speaking" activities** including pair and group work activities, increasing learner confidence when communicating in English.

SPEAKING

Comparing Three Natural Attractions

A | **Self-Reflection.** Discuss the questions with a partner.

1. How important is spending time in nature to you? Very important, somewhat important, or not very important? Explain.
2. Check (✔) the outdoor activities that you enjoy and add two more ideas of your own. Explain your choices to your partner.

   ❑ walking in a park or public garden   ❑ sitting near a river, lake, or ocean
   ❑ watching animals outdoors or at a zoo   ❑ other outdoor activities
   _____
   _____

B | Read the three advertisements for tours of natural attractions in South America.

IGUAZÚ FALLS
- Three days and two nights
- Visit the world's largest waterfall.
- Travel by plane from Buenos Aires to the Iguazú Falls.
- Go hiking in the national park and take beautiful photos from the observation areas.
- Enjoy a boat ride on the river below the falls.
- Stay in a luxury hotel.
- Cost: $750 per person

COLCA CANYON
- Two days and one night
- Travel by bus to the Pampas Cañahuas and see wild animals.
- See the amazing Colca Canyon, where it's possible to watch the Andean condor—the largest bird in the world.
- Stay in a small hotel in a village.
- Cost: $300 per person

GALÁPAGOS ISLANDS
- Four days and three nights
- Travel by boat to three islands where wild animals such as penguins, sea birds, and tortoises are common.
- Enjoy sunset walks on the famous Galápagos beaches.
- Stay in budget hotels on the islands and eat in the local restaurants (not included in the cost).
- Cost: $1200 per person

C | With your partner, decide which attraction you would like to visit together. Compare the attractions using the comparative and superlative form of the adjectives in the box and your own ideas. Say as many sentences as you can.

> The tour of the Colca Canyon is less expensive than the other two tours.

> That's true, but it's also the shortest tour.

amazing	expensive	interesting	short
beautiful	good	long	unusual

OUR RELATIONSHIP WITH NATURE | 171

The **"Viewing" section** works as a content-bridge between Lesson A and Lesson B and includes two pages of activities based on a fascinating video from National Geographic.

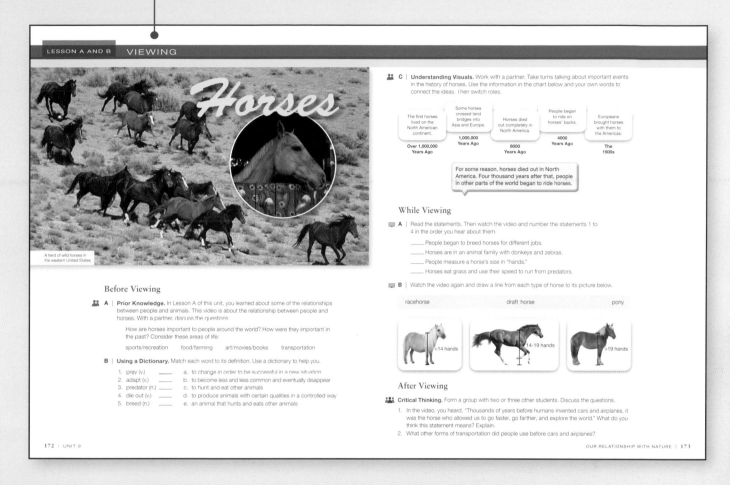

LESSON A AND B   VIEWING

Horses

A herd of wild horses in the western United States

Before Viewing

A | Prior Knowledge. In Lesson A of this unit, you learned about some of the relationships between people and animals. This video is about the relationship between people and horses. With a partner, discuss the questions.

How are horses important to people around the world? How were they important in the past? Consider these areas of life:

sports/recreation   food/farming   art/movies/books   transportation

B | Using a Dictionary. Match each word to its definition. Use a dictionary to help you.

1. prey (v.) _____   a. to change in order to be successful in a new situation
2. adapt (v.) _____ b. to become less and less common and eventually disappear
3. predator (n.) _____ c. to hunt and eat other animals
4. die out (v.) _____ d. to produce animals with certain qualities in a controlled way
5. breed (n.) _____   e. an animal that hunts and eats other animals

C | Understanding Visuals. Work with a partner. Take turns talking about important events in the history of horses. Use the information in the chart below and your own words to connect the ideas. Then switch roles.

The first horses lived on the North American continent.	Some horses crossed land bridges into Asia and Europe.	Horses died out completely in North America.	People began to ride on horses' backs.	Europeans brought horses with them to the Americas.
Over 1,000,000 Years Ago	1,000,000 Years Ago	8000 Years Ago	4000 Years Ago	The 1500s

For some reason, horses died out in North America. Four thousand years after that, people in other parts of the world began to ride horses.

While Viewing

A | Read the statements. Then watch the video and number the statements 1 to 4 in the order you hear about them.

_____ People began to breed horses for different jobs.
_____ Horses are in an animal family with donkeys and zebras.
_____ People measure a horse's size in "hands."
_____ Horses eat grass and use their speed to run from predators.

B | Watch the video again and draw a line from each type of horse to its picture below.

racehorse   draft horse   pony

<14 hands   14-19 hands   >19 hands

After Viewing

Critical Thinking. Form a group with two or three other students. Discuss the questions.

1. In the video, you heard, "Thousands of years before humans invented cars and airplanes, it was the horse who allowed us to go faster, go farther, and explore the world." What do you think this statement means? Explain.
2. What other forms of transportation did people use before cars and airplanes?

172 | UNIT 9

OUR RELATIONSHIP WITH NATURE | 173

● **A DVD for each level** contains 10 authentic videos from National Geographic specially adapted for English language learners.

NATIONAL GEOGRAPHIC LEARNING | HEINLE CENGAGE Learning

PATHWAYS 1
Listening, Speaking, and Critical Thinking

ISBN-13: 978-1-111-35044-4
ISBN-10: 1-111-35044-2

DVD
Total Running Time: 35:59

© 2012 National Geographic Learning, a part of Cengage Learning. ALL RIGHTS RESERVED.

A variety of activity types simulates the academic classroom where multiple skills must be applied simultaneously for success.

An **"Engage" section** at the end of the unit challenges learners with an end-of-unit presentation project. Speaking tips are offered for formal and informal group communication, instructing students to interact appropriately in different academic situations.

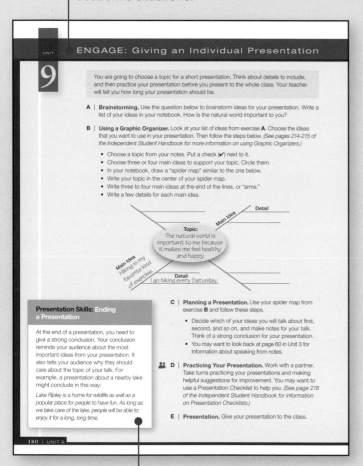

"Presentation Skills" boxes offer helpful tips and suggestions for successful academic presentations.

A 19-page **"Independent Student Handbook"** is conveniently located in the back of the book and provides helpful self-study strategies for students to become better independent learners.

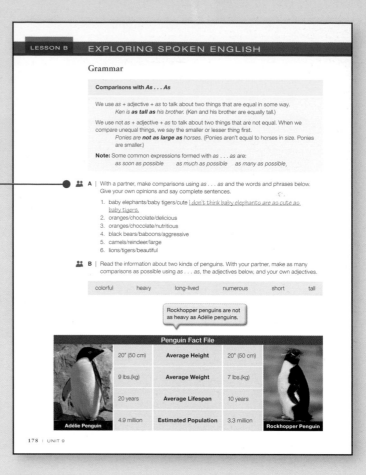

For the Teacher:

A **Teacher's Guide** is available in an easy-to-use format and includes teacher's notes, expansion activities, and answer keys for activities in the student book.

Perfect for integrating language practice with exciting visuals, **video clips from National Geographic** bring the sights and sounds of our world into the classroom.

The Assessment CD-ROM with ExamView® is a test-generating software program with a data bank of ready-made questions designed to allow teachers to assess students quickly and effectively.

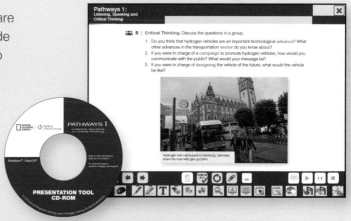

Bringing a new dimension to the language learning classroom, the **Classroom Presentation Tool CD-ROM** makes instruction clearer and learning easier through interactive activities, audio and video clips, and Presentation Worksheets.

For the Student:

The **Student Book** helps students achieve academic success in and outside of the classroom.

Audio CDs contain the audio recordings for the exercises in the student books.

ELT Powered by MyELT, the **Online Workbook** has both teacher-led and self-study options. It contains 10 National Geographic video clips, supported by interactive, automatically graded activities that practice the skills learned in the student books.

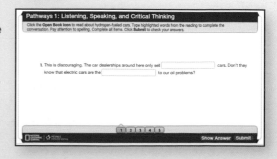

Visit elt.heinle.com/pathways for additional teacher and student resources.

CREDITS

LISTENING AND TEXT

17 Adapted from "Interview With Sylvia Earle (oceanographer)," http://kids.nationalgeographic.com/kids/stories/peopleplaces/sylvia-earle/: National Geographic Kids, **24** Adapted from "Funny Business," by David George Gordon: National Geographic World, April 1999, **35** Adapted from "City Parks: Space for the Soul," by Jennifer Ackerman: National Geographic Magazine, October 2006, **44** Adapted from "Searching for Cleopatra," by Marylou Tousignant: National Geographic Extreme Explorer, February 2011, **47** Adapted from "The Presence of the Past," by Allison Lassieur: National Geographic World, May 1998, **54** Adapted from "Tang Shipwreck," by Simon Worrall: National Geographic Magazine, June 2009, **55** Adapted from "Shipwreck in the Forbidden Zone," by Roff Smith: National Geographic Magazine, October 2009, **75-77** Adapted from "Viking Weather," by Tim Folger: National Geographic Magazine, June 2010, **79** Adapted from "Changing Rains," by Elizabeth Kolbert: National Geographic Magazine, April 2009, **84-87** Adapted from "Far-Out Foods," by Diane Wedner: National Geographic Explorer, November-December 2010, **90** Adapted from "Bugs as Food: Humans Bite" by Maryann Mott, National Geographic News, April 16, 2004, **94** Adapted from "Into the Heart of Dim Sum," by Jodi Helmer: National Geographic Traveler, March 2011, **94** Adapted from "Sweet Homecoming," by Jodi Helmer: National Geographic Traveler, March 2011

PHOTOS

1: Lynn Johnson/National Geographic Image Collection, **2:** Paul Chesley/National Geographic Image Collection, **2:** Ira Block /National Geographic Image Collection, **2:** Peter Stanley/National Geographic Image Collection, **3:** Alex Treadway/National Geographic Image Collection, **3:** Justin Guariglia/National Geographic, **3:** Frontpage/Shutterstock.com, **4:** Beverly Joubert/National Geographic Image Collection, **5:** William Allen/National Geographic Image Collection, **6:** Annie Griffiths/National Geographic Image Collection, **7:** Annie Griffiths/National Geographic Image Collection, **7:** Annie Griffiths/National Geographic Image Collection, **7:** Annie Griffiths/National Geographic Image Collection, **8:** Yuri Arcurs/Shutterstock.com, **8:** Catherine Yeulet/istockphoto.com, **10:** Rob Marmion/Shutterstock.com, **10:** Fritz Hoffman/National Geographic Image Collection, **10:** Mike Theiss/National Geographic Image Collection, **10:** Carsten Peter/Speleoresearch & Films/National Geographic Image Collection, **10:** Mike Theiss/National Geographic Image Collection, **11:** Moshimochi/Shutterstock.com, **11:** Andrey Novikov/Shutterstock.com, **11:** Gualtiero boffi/Shutterstock.com, **12:** Simon Marcus/Corbis Super RF/Alamy, **13:** Fancy/Veer/Corbis/Jupiter Images, **14:** Artistic Endeavor/Shutterstock.com, **14:** Michaeljung/Shutterstock.com, **14:** Rgerhardt/Shutterstock.com, **17:** Tyrone Turner/National Geographic Image Collection, **18:** Robert Adrian Hillman/Shutterstock.com, **19:** Vicki Reid/iStockphoto.com, **20:** Bob Daemmrich/Alamy, **21:** Bill Hatcher/National Geographic Image Collection, **22-23:** Ralph Lee Hopkins/National Geographic Image Collection, **23:** Lisa F. Young/Shutterstock.com, **23:** Stephan Zabel/iStockphoto.com, **23:** Joel Sartore/National Geographic Image Collection, **23:** Max blain/Shutterstock.com, **24:** Wesley Jenkins/iStockphoto.com, **25:** Joel Sartore/National Geographic Image Collection, **26:** StockLite/Shutterstock.com, **26:** Kristian sekulic/iStockphoto.com, **27:** James L. Stanfield/National Geographic Image Collection, **27:** Yagi Studio/Jupiter Images, **28:** National Geographic Image Collection, **29:** Julia Pivovarova/Shutterstock.com, **31:** Steve Raymer/National Geographic Image Collection, **31:** Joel Sartore/National Geographic Image Collection, **32:** Reuters/Thomas Mukoya /Landov, **32:** Hemis/Alamy, **32:** Georg Gerster/National Geographic Image Collection, **33:** Reuters/Thomas Mukoya /Landov, **34:** Huntstock/Photodisc /Jupiter Images, **34:** Huchen Lu/iStockphoto.com, **34:** Clerkenwell_Images/iStockphoto.com, **34:** Flashon Studio/Shutterstock.com, **35:** Amy Toensing/National Geographic Image Collection, **35:** Catherine Karnow/National Geographic Image Collection, **36:** Michael S. Yamashita/National Geographic Image Collection, **37:** Diane Cook and Len Jenshel/National Geographic Image Collection, **38:** Agnieszka Kirinicjanow/iStockphoto.com, **39:** Gerd Ludwig/National Geographic Image Collection, **41:** Bill Curtsinger/National Geographic Image Collection, **42-43:** Tim Laman/National Geographic Image Collection, **43:** Bates Littlehales/National Geographic Image Collection, **43:** Don Kincaid/National Geographic Image Collection, **43:** Jonathan Blair/National Geographic Image Collection, **44:** Raj Singh/Alamy, **44:** George Steinmetz/National Geographic Image Collection, **45:** Javarman/Shutterstock.com, **47:** AP Photo/Ben Curtis, **49:** Catherine Karnow/National Geographic Image Collection, **50:** David Mclain/National Geographic Image Collection, **50:** Interfoto/Alamy, **51:** Emory Kristof/National Geographic Image Collection, **52:** Ira Block/National Geographic Image Collection, **52:** S Murphy-Larronde/Age fotostock/Photolibrary, **52:** George Oze/Alamy, **53:** Dominik Dabrowski/Istockphoto.com, **53:** Arena Creative/Shutterstock.com, **53:** K.L. Kohn/Shutterstock.com, **55:** Tony Law/National Geographic Image Collection, **57:** Tony Law/National Geographic Image Collection, **58:** Harris & Ewing Collection/Library of Congress, **59:** Branislav Senic/Shutterstock.com, **60:** Bill Aron/PhotoEdit, **61:** Mike Theiss/National Geographic Image Collection, **62:** Paul Chesley/National Geographic Image Collection, **62:** Jason Edwards/National Geographic Image Collection, **62:** Jodi Cobb/National Geographic Image Collection, **62:** Jim Lopes/Shutterstock.com, **62:** Vlasov Pavel /Shutterstock.com, **62-63:** Kevin Mcelheran/National Geographic Image Collection, **64:** Petr Bukal/Shutterstock.com, **64:** Galyna Andrushko/Shutterstock.com, **66:** James P. Blair/National Geographic Image Collection, **66:** Sergey_Ryzhenko/Shutterstock.com, **66:** Ellen McKnight/Alamy, **67:** Vlad Siaber/Shutterstock.com, **69:** Grady Reese/iStockphoto.com, **70:** Rich Reid/National Geographic Image Collection, **71:** Tyler Olson/Shutterstock.com, **72:** Mike Theiss/National Geographic Image Collection, **73:** Carsten Peter/National Geographic Image Collection, **73:** Robert Clark/National Geographic Image Collection, **73:** MikeTheiss/National Geographic Image Collection, **74:** Janina Dierks/Shutterstock.com, **74:** NASA Goddard Space Flight Center (NASA-GSFC), **74:** Rita Januskeviciute/Shutterstock.com, **74:** Peter Essick/National Geographic Image Collection, **76:** Peter Essick/National Geographic Image Collection, **77:** Peter Essick/National Geographic Image Collection, **78:** ilker canikligil/iStockphoto.com, **78:** cstar55/iStockphoto.com, **80:** acilo/iStockphoto.com, **81:** Manoocher/National Geographic Image Collection, **82:** Nicole Duplaix/National Geographic Image Collection, **82:** Eye Ubiquitous/Glowimages.com, **82:** Elena Elisseeva/Shutterstock.com, **82:** Gordon Wiltsie/National Geographic Image Collection, **82:** Don Tran/Shutterstock.com, **82:** David Doubilet/National Geographic Image Collection, **82-83:** George Steinmetz/National Geographic Image Collection, **84:** Mark Doherty/Shutterstock.com, **84:** Muellek Josef/Shutterstock.com, **84:** whethervain/iStockphoto.com, **85:** Mark Thiessen/National Geographic Image Collection, **86:** Chico Sanchez/Alamy, **86:** Aaron Huey/National Geographic Image Collection, **87:** Jakub Pavlinec/Shutterstock.com, **89:** Lisa F. Young/Shutterstock.com, **90:** Joel Sartore/National Geographic Image Collection, **91:** Gina Martin/National Geographic Image Collection, **91:** phloen/Shutterstock.com, **91:** Maria Dryfhout/Shutterstock.com, **91:** Elena Elisseeva/iStockphoto.com, **91:** Nataliya_Ostapenko/Shutterstock.com, **92:** Michael Durham/Minden Pictures, **93:** Neil McAllister/Alamy, **93:** Michael Durham/Minden Pictures, **94:** 4kodiak/iStockphoto.com, **94:** Stephen Harrison/Alamy, **94:** elena moiseeva/Shutterstock.com, **95:** Catherine Karnow /National Geographic Image Collection, **95:** Stephen Alvarez/National Geographic Image Collection, **96:** Stephen Alvarez/National Geographic Image Collection, **97:** John Giustina/Riser/Getty Images, **98:** RoJo Images,2010/Shutterstock.com, **98:** Christopher Paquette/Istockphoto.com, **98:** Justin Guariglia/National Geographic Image Collection, **98:** Nayashkova Olga/Shutterstock.com, **100:** 54613/Shutterstock.com, **100:** Luiz Rocha/Shutterstock.com, **100:** Jordan Tan/Shutterstock.com

MAP AND ILLUSTRATION

2-3: National Geographic Maps; **32:** National Geographic Maps, **32:** National Geographic Maps; **45:** National Geographic Maps; **46:** National Geographic Maps; **52:** National Geographic Maps; **54:** Fernando G. Baptista/National Geographic Magazine; **75:** National Geographic Magazine Maps; **79:** Sean McNaughton/National Geographic Magazine; **92:** National Geographic Maps; **208:** Bob Kayganich/illustrationonline; **216:** National Geographic Maps

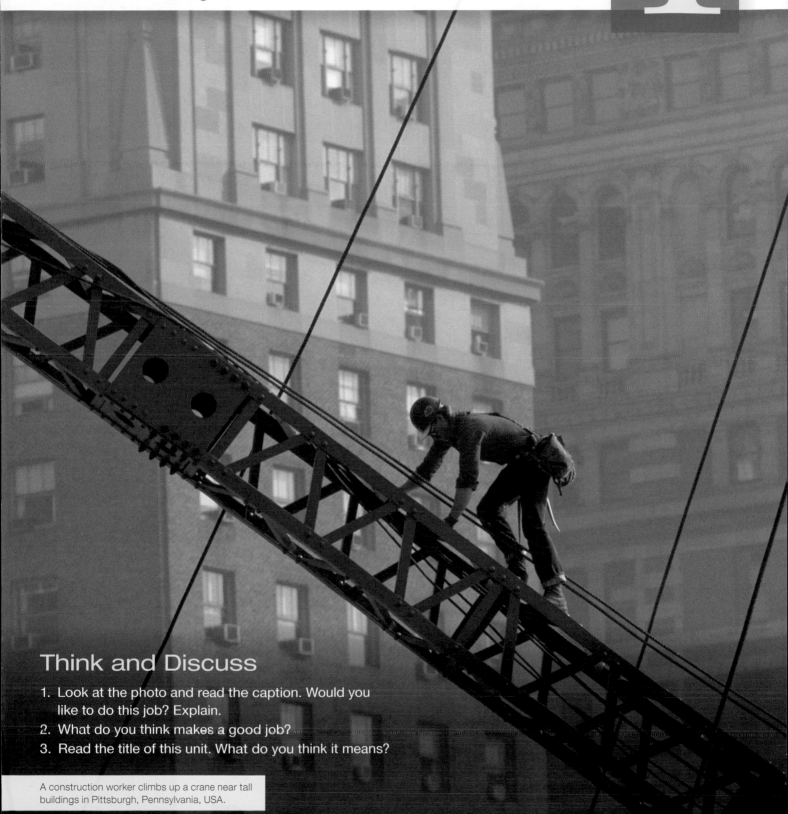

Living for Work

ACADEMIC PATHWAYS
Lesson A: Listening to an Interview
Doing an Interview
Lesson B: Listening to an Informal Conversation
Giving a Short Presentation about Yourself

Think and Discuss

1. Look at the photo and read the caption. Would you like to do this job? Explain.
2. What do you think makes a good job?
3. Read the title of this unit. What do you think it means?

A construction worker climbs up a crane near tall buildings in Pittsburgh, Pennsylvania, USA.

Exploring the Theme: Living for Work

Look at the photos and read the captions. Match the photos with the places on the map. Then discuss the questions.

1. Which job looks the most interesting? Explain.
2. Which job do you think is the most difficult? Explain.
3. Which jobs would you like to do? Explain.

a

Firefighters put out fires and help people. Their work is very dangerous, so they need to learn special skills. This firefighter works in New York City, **USA**.

b

Policemen and **policewomen** help people in many different ways. Some police officers ride horses when they work. This **policewoman** is from **Canada**.

c

Farmers usually work outdoors. They need to know how to plant and grow food. These farmers in **Ethiopia** are harvesting wheat.

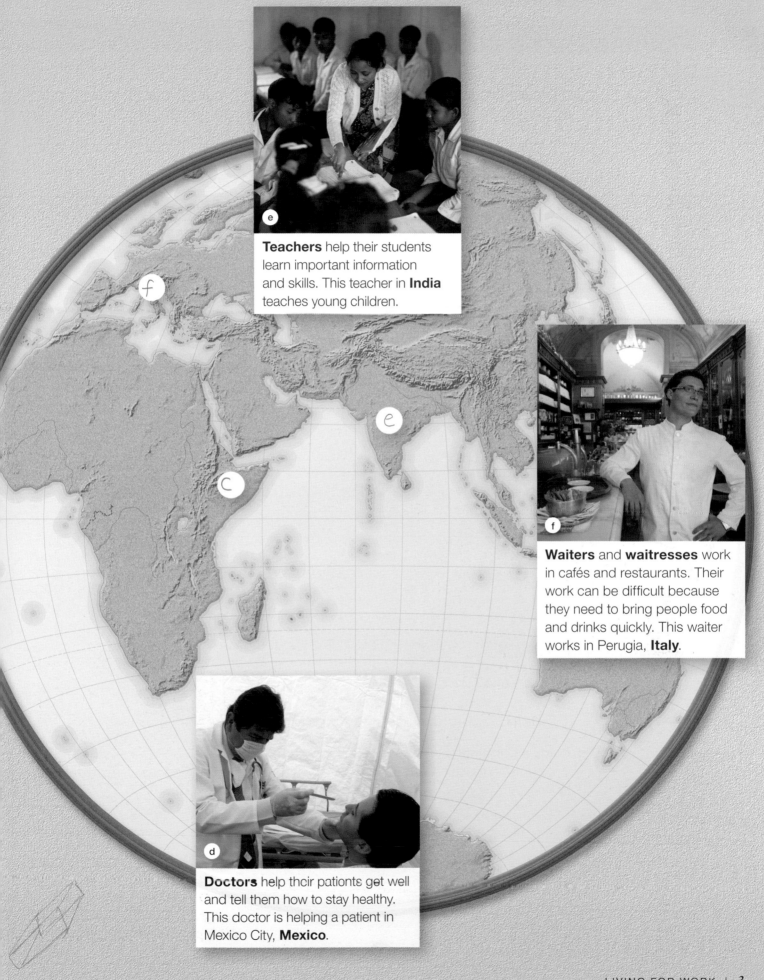

Teachers help their students learn important information and skills. This teacher in **India** teaches young children.

Waiters and **waitresses** work in cafés and restaurants. Their work can be difficult because they need to bring people food and drinks quickly. This waiter works in Perugia, **Italy**.

Doctors help their patients get well and tell them how to stay healthy. This doctor is helping a patient in Mexico City, **Mexico**.

homework

A | Using a Dictionary. Read and listen to the words. Then match each word with its definition. These are words you will hear and use in Lesson A.

1. _c_ travel   a. (n.) a chance to do something
2. _a_ opportunity   b. (adj.) likely to hurt or harm you
3. _d_ experiences   c. (v.) to go from one place to another
4. _e_ skills   d. (n.) things you do or that happen to you
5. _b_ dangerous   e. (n.) things you are able to do well

B | Meaning from Context. Read and listen to the article. Notice the words in **blue**. These are words you will hear and use in Lesson A.

Dereck and Beverly Joubert filming and photographing a meerkat in Africa.

Beverly and Dereck Joubert

Beverly Joubert and her husband Dereck are **creative** people. Together, they write and make interesting films about animals in Africa. They love to **explore** different parts of Africa, and the result is 22 films, 10 books, and many articles!

In order to work together, the Jouberts need to **communicate** well and understand one another. Their films win many awards[1], but for the Jouberts, making films is an **adventure**. It is also a way to do something good for endangered[2] animals. They started the Big Cats Initiative fund[3]. With this money, the Jouberts can **help** the lions and other animals they love. Says Dereck, "If there was ever a time to take action, it is now."

[1]An **award** is a prize for doing something well.
[2]Something that is **endangered** might soon disappear or become extinct.
[3]A **fund** is money to be used for a certain purpose.

**C | Write each word in blue from exercise B next to its definition.

1. ___creative___ (adj.) having imagination and artistic ability
2. _explore_ (v.) to go different places and learn about things
3. _adventure_ (n.) an exciting time or event
4. _communicate_ (v.) to share information with others
5. _help_ (v.) to do something good for someone or something

D | Using a Dictionary. Work with a partner. Complete the chart with other forms of the words from exercises **A** and **B**. Use your dictionary to help you. (*See page 208 of the Independent Student Handbook for more information on using a dictionary.*)

Noun	Verb	Adjective
exploration	explore	exploratory
Communiction	communicate	Communcative
help	help	helping / helpful
Creation	Create	creative

A | Work with a partner. Read the conversation and fill in each blank with a word from the box. Then practice the conversation.

communicate	creative	explore	help	opportunity

A: Guess what! I have a new job (1) _opportunity_

B: That's great! What's the job?

A: I get to go to Kenya and take photos for a book. It's pretty (2) _creative_ work, and I can (3) _explore_ Kenya while I'm there.

B: Good for you! Can you (4) _communicate_ by email or telephone from there?

A: Oh, sure. I can send you an email message every day.

B: Good. Then I won't worry about you.

A: By the way, can you (5) _help_ me with something now?

B: No problem. What do you need?

A: I need you to pick up my camera from the camera shop.

 B | Read the article. Then fill in each blank with a word from the box. Use each word only once. Then listen and check your answers.

track 1-4

adventure	dangerous	experiences	skills	travel

Photographer Annie Griffiths

Annie Griffiths is famous for her beautiful photographs. The photos come from countries all over the world, so it's just a normal part of life for Griffiths to (1) _travel_.

Living in other countries is not for everyone, but for Griffiths and her children, it's an (2) _adventure_. Her children especially love the Middle East, and their (3) _experiences_ in that part of the world helped them to learn about other cultures.

Griffiths' work can also be (4) _dangerous_. Traveling is not always safe. In the Galápagos Islands, Griffiths found herself in the water with sharks one day!

Besides writing and taking pictures, Griffiths teaches photography (5) _skills_ to people who want to become photographers. They know they are learning from one of the best photographers in the world.

Photographer Annie Griffiths on location in Petra, Jordan

Before Listening

Predicting Content. You are going to listen to an interview with Annie Griffiths. Look at the photo and information. What do you think Griffiths will talk about? Discuss your ideas with a partner.

About My Photo

Where: Victoria Falls, Zambia

When: around sunset, in 2006

What: a swimmer

Why: beautiful light, amazing place

Listening: An Interview

Critical Thinking Focus: Identifying Main Ideas

The main idea or ideas of a talk are the speaker's most important ideas. The details of a talk give more information about the main ideas.

a swimmer realy Travil

track 1-5 **A | Listening for Main Ideas.** Listen to an interview with Annie Griffiths. Check (✔) the main idea of the interview.

❏ Annie Griffiths' work is dangerous sometimes.

☑ Annie Griffiths' job as a photographer is very interesting.

❏ Annie Griffiths knows how to communicate with the people she meets.

track 1-5 **B | Listening for Details.** Read the statements and answer choices. Then listen to the interview again and choose the correct word or phrase.

1. Annie Griffiths' favorite place is _____.
   a. New Zealand
   b. The Middle East
   c. Southern Africa

2. Annie Griffiths loves taking pictures of wildlife and _____.
   a. landscapes
   b. beaches
   c. cities

Travil

3. Annie Griffiths took her children with her because her assignments were _____.
   a. two or three months long
   b. three or four months long
   c. four or five months long

4. When Annie Griffiths doesn't know the local language, she gestures and _____.
   a. writes
   b. smiles
   c. translates

5. Annie Griffiths describes the day she took the photo at Victoria Falls as _____.
   a. hot and humid
   b. unforgettable
   c. adventurous

Annie Griffiths' children in Petra, Jordan, wearing Bedouin clothing and pretending to drink tea.

After Listening

A | Making Inferences. Read the statements and circle **T** for *true* or **F** for *false*. The answers are not in the speakers' exact words. You need to think about what you heard.

1. Annie Griffiths likes her life of adventure.   **T**   **F**
2. Griffiths knows how to make friends with strangers.   **T**   **F**
3. Griffiths does not go to places that are dangerous.   **T**   **F**
4. Griffiths' children do not like to travel.   **T**   **F**

B | Self-Reflection. Discuss the questions with a partner.

1. Griffiths takes her children to work. Is it a good idea to take your family to work? Explain.
2. What places do you like to travel to? What do you think is fun and interesting about traveling?

Ancient acacia trees grow near the huge red sand dunes of the Namib Desert. Photo by Annie Griffiths

Galápagos sea lions resting on a white beach. Photo by Annie Griffiths

Almost

Jordan

Do they need

Language Function

Communicating that You Don't Understand

We use these expressions and others to communicate that we don't understand what someone says. *(See pages 210-211 of the Independent Student Handbook for more information on useful phrases and expressions.)*

I don't understand.	*I'm sorry?*	*I'm not sure what you mean.*
Do you mean . . .?	*I'm sorry, I missed that.*	

 A | Read and listen to the conversation. Then <u>underline</u> the expressions that show when the speakers don't understand.

track 1-6

A: I took a job aptitude test today.

B: A job aptitude test? What's that?

A: Well, it's a test of your skills and interests.

B: I see. And did you get the job?

A: I'm not sure what you mean.

B: I mean—you took a job test, right? Did you do well on the test and get the job?

A: Oh, no. The test only shows which job might be good for you.

B: Ah, I see. It helps you to choose the right job.

A: Exactly!

what dose mean

 B | Practice the conversation from exercise **A** with a partner. Then switch roles and practice it again.

bui

 C | Practice the conversations below with your partner. Student B uses one of the expressions from the box. Then switch roles and practice the conversations again using different expressions.

1. **A:** You need a lot of special skills to be a builder.
   B: ...I'm not sure what you mean.
   A: Well, to build houses, you need to know how to do many things.

2. **A:** Being a teacher is an adventure.
   B: ...Do you you mean
   A: Every day in the classroom is different. You never know what will happen.

Grammar

The Simple Present vs. The Present Continuous

We use the *simple present* for:
1. Repeated actions or habits: *He **goes** to work at eight o'clock every day.*
2. Things that are always true: *Fish **swim** in the ocean.*

Note: We use an -s ending with third person singular verbs in the simple present.

> *It/She/He always **arrives** late.*

We use the *present continuous* for:
1. Things that are happening now: *She is **taking** a photo.*
2. Things that are happening around this time: *I **am traveling** a lot these days.*

A | Read the conversations below. Fill in each blank with the simple present or the present continuous form of a verb from the box. You will need to use one verb twice.

cook	help	sell	show	teach	text	~~work~~	write

Peter: What do you do, Jorge?

Jorge: I (1) ____work____ in a restaurant.

Peter: What are you doing right now?

Jorge: I (2) _____ a new meal for tonight.

Peter: Smells delicious.

Brenda: Hi, Steve. What are you working on?

Steve: I (3) _____ a new computer program.

Brenda: Sounds fun.

Cho: You're a real estate agent, right Raquel?

Raquel: Yes, that's right. I (4) _____ and (5) _____ homes.
I (6) _____ a house to a buyer at the moment.

Lana: What are you doing on your smartphone?

Dennis: I (7) _____ Bill.

Lana: Bill?

Dennis: You know, Professor Bill Franks. He (8) _____ right now.
Hopefully he can meet us after his lecture.

Eduardo: What do you do for your job?

Frank: I'm a police officer. I (9) _____ people who are in trouble.

👥 **B** | Work with a partner. Look at the photo. Then read the story and fill in each blank with the verb in parentheses. Use the simple present or present continuous.

This is Cynthia Lauber and her son Mark. Cynthia (1) _____works_____ (work) in a clothing store in Lincoln, Nebraska, in the United States. She (2) _____ (help) people find the right clothes. Unfortunately, Cynthia (3) _____ (not make) much money at the store. She (4) _____ (look) for a different job. At the moment, Mark (5) _____ (help) her search for jobs online. They (6) _____ (make) a list of possibilities, but Cynthia (7) _____ (not have) the skills for every job.

👥 **C** | With your partner, look at the photos. Then answer the questions and discuss the different jobs.

In which job   . . . do you explore different places?

. . . do you need good communication skills?

. . . do you travel a lot?

. . . do you help people?

. . . do you need special skills?

Chef

Fisherman

Reporter

Construction Worker

👥 **D** | **Discussion.** Work with your partner. Follow the instructions below.

1. Look around the room. Talk about three things that are happening in the room right now.
2. Think of someone you know well. Tell your partner three things that person is probably doing right now.
3. Think of a job you both know about. Make a list of three things a person with that job does every day.

Doing an Interview

👥 **A** | **Note-Taking.** Work with a partner. Take turns asking and answering the questions from the Career Aptitude Test. Take short notes on your partner's answers.

Career Aptitude Test	
A career aptitude test can help you decide which job or career is right for you.	
Interview Questions	**My Partner's Answers**
1. Are you a creative person?	I think so
2. Do you like to travel and explore new places?	Yeah
3. Are you afraid of dangerous situations? For example, working with animals or with electricity?	No
4. Do you have good communication skills?	Yes
5. Do you like to spend time with other people, or do you prefer to spend time alone?	with other people
6. Do you like to keep fit?	Yeah
7. Are you a good problem-solver?	Yes
8. Do you like to help people?	Yes i like

News reporters have good communication skills.

Computer programmers are good problem-solvers.

Teachers like to help people.

👥 **B** | Look back at your notes from exercise **A**. Then tell your partner which jobs in the box below might be good for him or her. Explain your reasons.

business executive	doctor/nurse	firefighter	photographer	salesperson
computer programmer	farmer	news reporter	restaurant worker	teacher

👥 **C** | Form a group with another pair of students and follow the steps below.

1. Tell the group which job might be best for your partner. Explain your reasons.
2. Tell the group your opinion of your partner's choice of job for you. Is it really a good job for you? Why, or why not?

living for work

BUTLER SCHOOL

Before Viewing

A | Prior Knowledge. Look at the photo of a butler. Then read each sentence and circle **T** for *true* or **F** for *false*.

1. Butlers usually work in England.		**T**	**F**
2. Butlers work for rich people in large houses.		**T**	**F**
3. Butlers wear informal clothes.		**T**	**F**
4. Butlers speak in a formal way.		**T**	**F**

B | Using a Dictionary. Match each word from the video to its definition. Use your dictionary to help you.

1. refreshments (n.) ____   a. to go and get something
2. fetch (v.) ____   b. to do something again and again in order to improve
3. practice (v.) ____   c. a custom or belief that has existed for a long time
4. tradition (n.) ____   d. things to drink or eat

While Viewing

A | Watch the video. Circle the correct word or phrase for each sentence.

1. In the past, there were (many/few) butlers.
2. Nowadays, there are (many/few) butlers.
3. The students at the school come from (one country/many countries).
4. Butler school is (easy/difficult) for the students.

B | Using the Simple Present. Watch the video again. Check (✔) the things students do at the butler school.

❏ graduate from the school   ❏ learn to walk correctly
❏ iron newspapers   ❏ practice saying things
❏ learn from books   ❏ wash clothes

After Viewing

 A | **Discussion.** With a partner, read the list of careers and the words and phrases in the box below. Then discuss each career using some of the words and phrases from the box and your own ideas.

> I think doctors work very long hours.

> That's true, but they make a high salary.

Careers:

butler	news reporter
businessperson	scientist
doctor	waiter/waitress

dangerous	high salary	low pay
difficult job	interesting work	opportunities to learn new things
easy work	long hours	travel opportunities

B | **Critical Thinking.** Read the two advertisements for career schools. Then with your partner, follow the steps below.

Learn to be a Medical Assistant!

Doctors and nurses are not the only people in a hospital. Medical assistants work in:

- Medical offices
- Medical laboratories

At Liverton Technical College, students receive six weeks of interesting classes and three weeks of training at a hospital.

To learn more about this exciting career, call or email now: (963) 555-4362; info@LT.com

---

APT School for the Culinary Arts since 1952

At APT, food and restaurants are everything. Choose from the following 16-week courses:

- *Head Chef*
- *Dessert Chef*
- *Food Server*
- *Dining Room Manager*

You could soon have a career as a restaurant worker! Call or email today. (217) 555-7090; chef@apt.com

---

1. Use some of the words and phrases from exercise **A** to describe the careers in the advertisements: medical assistant and restaurant worker.
2. Tell your partner which career might be better for you. Explain your reasons.
3. Tell your partner which career-school advertisement you think is better and why.

English
Speeker

 A | **Meaning from Context.** Read and listen to three interviews. Notice the words in blue. These are words you will hear and use in Lesson B.

track 1-7

Q: What kind of people make good nurses?

A: Well, you have to be **organized**. For example, I'm **in charge of** my patients' medicine. I have to give them the correct medicine, so I write everything down in a chart. I get the medicine. Then, I check on my chart that it's the correct one. Nobody gets the wrong medicine that way.

Q: You *are* well organized!

A: Thanks. It has a big **effect** on my patients' health, so it's important to me. Nurses also have to be fit because the work is very **physical**.

Q: What kind of physical work do you do?

A: I stand or walk all the time, and sometimes I have to lift patients up from their beds.

Q: Is teaching a difficult job?

A: Sometimes it is. **Although** the students are wonderful, the school has a rule I don't like.

Q: What kind of rule?

A: Well, I teach math and science, and I think they're very important subjects. But students here don't have to take both subjects. They can take one or the other and still **graduate**.

Q: Do you mean they can finish school and never take math, for example?

A: Yes, they can. It's not a good idea, in my opinion.

Q: What does an engineer do every day?

A: Well, there are many kinds of engineers. I'm an industrial engineer. I look at our processes here at the factory, and I **search** for any problems.

Q: What do you do if you find a problem?

A: I give a **presentation** to my **managers**. We have a meeting, and I explain the problem to them. We try to find ways to solve it.

Q: What happens next?

A: They usually follow my suggestions.

Q: So the managers here have a lot of respect for you.

A: Yes, I **believe** they do respect me. It's one of the reasons I like my job.

Kind
like
but

B | **Using a Dictionary.** Check (✔) the words you already know or understand from the context in exercise **A**. Use a dictionary to help you with any words you are unsure of.

☑ although (conj.)   ☑ in charge of (phrase)   ☑ graduate (v.)   ☑ organized (adj.)   ☑ presentation (n.)
☑ believe (v.)   ☑ effect (n.)   ☑ managers (n.)   ☑ physical (adj.)   ☑ search (v.)

USING VOCABULARY

homework

A | Complete each sentence with a word from the box.

although	effect	graduate	physical	presentations	search

1. It's a good job, _althoμgh_ the salary is not very high.
2. Roland needs to _search_ for a new job.
3. He speaks well and gives good business _presentations_.
4. Each year more than 4000 students _graduate_ from the school.
5. They exercise and they're very fit, so they can do very _physical_ work.
6. A good manager can have a positive _effect_ on the employees' work.

B | Read the conversation. Then fill in each blank with a word or phrase from the box.

although	believe	graduated	in charge of	organized

Interviewer: So, you (1) _believe_ a creative job is the best thing for you?

Jenny: Yes, I do. I (2) _graduated_ from college with a degree in photography.

Interviewer: What other job skills do you have?

Jenny: Well, I'm very (3) _organized_. At my last job we moved offices. I managed the move. I had to make sure everything arrived in the new office.

Interviewer: Can you manage other employees?

Jenny: Yes. In my last job I was (4) _in charge of_ five other employees. (5) _although_ it was hard work, I enjoyed it a lot.

C | **Role-Playing.** Work with a partner. Role-play the situation below. Then switch roles.

Student A: You are the manager at a workplace. Ask your partner the job interview questions from the conversation in exercise **B**.

Student B: You are at a job interview. You really want the job. Answer the interview questions with your own ideas.

D | **Critical Thinking.** Discuss the questions with your partner.

1. What **effect** does each worker in exercise **A** on page 14 have on the world? For example, what **effect** does the nurse have on her patients' health?
2. What does the engineer **believe** about his **managers**? Do you think he is right? Explain.
3. Besides nursing, what other jobs are very **physical**? Are they good jobs in your opinion?
4. In what ways are you an **organized** student? How could you be more **organized**?

Pronunciation

Syllable Stress
We can divide words in English into one or more syllables. For example, *doctor* has two syllables (doc-tor). In words with more than one syllable, one syllable usually receives the main stress. For example, in the word doctor, *doc* is stressed. The syllable with the main stress is louder and longer than the other syllables.
Examples:

track 1-8

One syllable:	Two syllables:	Three syllables:
book	**doc**-tor	**com**-pan-y

 track 1-9

A | Listen and <u>underline</u> the main stress in each word.

one

1. nur<u>se</u>
2. <u>stu</u>dy
3. <u>tra</u>vel
4. re<u>mem</u>ber
5. re<u>por</u>ter
6. cre<u>a</u>tive
7. re<u>ceive</u>
8. <u>skills</u>

 track 1-10

B | Write each word from the box in the correct column of the chart below. Then listen and check your answers.

| ③ adventure | ① cook | ① know | ③ officer | ② travel |
| ③ amazing | fly ① | ② money | ② teacher | ③ yesterday |

One-syllable Words	Two-syllable Words	Three-syllable Words
cook	money	adventure

Before Listening

 track 1-11

Here are some words you will hear in the Listening section. Listen and repeat the words. Then answer the questions below.

billion	marine biologist	ocean	pollution	tuna

1. How many syllables are in each word? Write the number of syllables next to each word.
2. Which syllable in each word receives the most stress? <u>Underline</u> the syllables with the most stress.

Listening: An Informal Conversation

A | You are going to listen to a conversation between two students. Listen to the first part of the conversation. What are the students talking about? Check (✔) the correct answer.

❏ a presentation that Becca missed
❏ a presentation that Franco missed
❏ a presentation that was not very good

B | **Listening for Main Ideas.** Listen to the entire conversation. Check (✔) the main idea of the conversation.

❏ Becca was not in class on Thursday because she was sick.
❏ The presentation was very good.
❏ Dr. Earle says the world's people are having a bad effect on the oceans.

C | **Listening for Details.** Listen again. Check (✔) any ideas that are NOT part of the conversation.

❏ Becca feels better today.
❏ Dr. Earle gave a presentation to the class on Thursday.
❏ Dr. Earle earns a high salary.
❏ There are almost seven billion people on earth now.
❏ It's fine to eat tuna and other large ocean fish.

Dr. Sylvia Earle

After Listening

A | **Self-Reflection.** Read each statement below and circle *Agree* or *Disagree*.

1. Dr. Earle's career might be a good career for me.	**Agree**	**Disagree**
2. When you're sick, it's better not to go to class.	**Agree**	**Disagree**
3. The large number of people in the world is a problem.	**Agree**	**Disagree**
4. What people eat has a big effect on the oceans.	**Agree**	**Disagree**

Student to Student: Giving Feedback while Listening

Use these expressions to show someone that you're listening and interested in the conversation.

Really? I see. *Interesting!* *I see what you mean.* *Wow!*

B | **Discussion.** Form a group with two or three other students. Discuss the statements in exercise **A**. Give reasons why you agree or disagree with each statement. Use the expressions from the box to show interest in your classmates' ideas.

Grammar

 A | Work with a partner. Practice the conversation. Then switch roles and practice it again.

Terry:	What are you doing, Chris?
Chris:	I'm writing in my journal.
Terry:	Interesting! How often do you do that?
Chris:	Well, I always write something before I go to bed.
Terry:	And you sometimes write during the day, too—like you're doing now.
Chris:	That's right. Are you surprised?
Terry:	A little bit. People are usually on their smartphones and laptops nowadays. I seldom see anyone writing in a journal.
Chris:	I guess I'm strange, but you probably knew that already.
Terry:	Very funny. You might be a little strange, but in a *good* way.
Chris:	Thanks, Terry.

 B | **Discussion.** With your partner, discuss the questions about the conversation from exercise **A**.

1. Does Chris write in his journal every night? How do you know?
2. Does Chris write in his journal every day? How do you know?
3. Does Terry see people writing in a journal very often? How do you know?

Adverbs of Frequency

We use adverbs of frequency to talk about how often we do things. These adverbs go before most verbs, but after the verb *be*.

> I **always** <u>brush</u> my teeth in the morning.
> This bus <u>is</u> **usually** on time.

100%	**always**	*My children **always** do their homework.*
	usually	*That photographer **usually** takes good pictures.*
	often	*Archaeologists are **often** outdoors.*
	sometimes	*My uncle **sometimes** gives me money.*
	occasionally	*The weather here is **occasionally** very hot.*
	rarely/seldom	*Lorna is rarely in the library. She **seldom** works there.*
0%	**never**	*I am **never** late for class.*

C | Complete each sentence with an appropriate adverb of frequency. There may be more than one correct answer.

1. Butlers _____ wear formal clothes at work.
2. Annie Griffiths _____ takes beautiful photos.
3. Good students _____ forget to do their homework.
4. Doctors _____ work at more than one hospital.
5. Marine biologists _____ swim in the ocean.
6. Archaeologists _____ work indoors.

D | Compare your answers from exercise **C** with a partner's. When you have different answers, compare the meanings of the adverbs of frequency.

Language Function: Using Adverbs of Frequency

A | Work with a partner. Read the work schedule of a hotel housekeeper named Erica. Then answer the questions below.

1. Which days does Erica work at the hotel? Which days does she not work?
2. Which day is Erica's longest workday? Which is the shortest?
3. What does Erica have to do for her job?

B | With your partner, discuss Erica's weekly schedule using adverbs of frequency. Use the language from exercise **A** and your own ideas.

Hotel Avalon

Weekly work schedule: Erica S.

Tuesday	Wednesday	Thursday	Friday	Saturday
start: 7:00 a.m.	start: 7:00 a.m.	start: 7:00 a.m.	start: 7:00 a.m.	start: 7:00 a.m.
				end: 12:00 p.m.
end: 3:30 p.m.	end: 3:30 p.m.		end: 3:30 p.m.	
		end: 5:30 p.m.		

Job Duties:
Every day: *clean the guest bathrooms; make beds; remove trash*
Tuesday through Friday: *get clean sheets and towels from the hotel laundry room*
Wednesday and Friday: *clean the restaurant dining room after breakfast*
Saturday: *put new menus and information cards in the guest rooms*

> Erica always starts work early in the morning.

> Erica never works in the hotel kitchen.

C | **Discussion.** Form a group with two or three other students. Discuss which words you might use to describe Erica's job. Then think of two more words that describe her job.

dangerous	difficult	easy
high-paying	interesting	physical

You are going to introduce yourself and give a short presentation about yourself.

A | Planning a Presentation. Write your answers to the questions in the chart below or in your notebook. Then share your answers with a partner.

Questions	Answers
1. What's your name (the name you want to be called in this class)?	Abdullah
2. Where are you from?	Saudi Ariabia
3. What subjects are you studying?	English
4. What do you like to do in your free time?	watching movie
5. What is one interesting fact about you?	Play soccer

Presentation Skills: Introducing Yourself

When you give a presentation, you can use these expressions to introduce yourself.

Hi, I'm (your name).   *Hello, my name is (your name).*
I'm from (your city, country, university, etc.)

B | Planning a Presentation Read and listen to one student's presentation. Then follow the steps below.

track 1-14

I like +

interesting it is an aid

Hi, everyone. My name is Alejandro, but please call me Alex. I'm from Bogotá. As you know, that's the capital city of Colombia. I'm studying English now, and I'm also studying international relations. In my free time, I like to play tennis or send text messages to my friends. One interesting fact about me is that I have a pretty large family. I live with my parents, two sisters and one brother, and two grandparents as well.

1. Underline the expressions Alex uses to introduce himself.
2. Circle the information Alex gives about the place he's from.
3. Decide which expressions you will use to introduce yourself.

C | Presentation. Introduce yourself to the class or to a small group. Then tell them about yourself using the information from exercise **A**. You can use the student's presentation from exercise **B** to help you.

Good Times, Good Feelings

ACADEMIC PATHWAYS
Lesson A: Listening to a Lecture
          Discussing Celebrations and Holidays
Lesson B: Listening to a Talk with Questions and Answers
          Giving a Presentation for a Small Group

Think and Discuss

1. Look at the photo. What is this man doing? Why?
2. How do you think the man in the photo feels?

A man greets the sun after several days of rain
at Mavora Lakes, South Island, New Zealand.

21

Exploring the Theme:
Good Times, Good Feelings

A | Look at the photos and read the captions. Then discuss the questions.

1. What activities make people feel good?
2. Do you do any of these activities? Do they make you feel good? Why, or why not?
3. What other activities make you feel good? Why?

King of
Lord of

LYNCHBUR
LEMONADE

Hot air balloons float above a crowd at a Balloon
Fiesta, Albuquerque, New Mexico, USA.

Research says that when we **help other people**, we feel good.

We feel good when we do **physical exercise**.

Having **close friendships and family connections** makes us feel good.

Having regular **vacations** and **time away from work** helps us feel good.

🎧 **A** | Listen and check (✔) the words you already know. These are words you will hear and use in Lesson A.

track 1-15

❑ funny (adj.)	❑ joy (n.)	❑ led (v.)	❑ recorded (v.)	❑ situations (n.)
❑ joke (n.)	❑ laughter (n.)	❑ noise (n.)	❑ researchers (n.)	❑ unique (adj.)

🎧 **B** | **Meaning from Context.** Read and listen to the article and notice the words in blue.

track 1-16

a chimpanzee

From Pant-Pant to Ha-Ha

Look at the photo. Does this look like laughter? New research says that apes laugh when they are tickled[1]. **Researchers** at the University of Portsmouth **led** a 'tickle team.' The group of researchers tickled the necks, feet, hands, and armpits of young apes. The team **recorded** more than 800 of the resulting laughs on tape. The research suggests that the apes' panting[2] **noise** is the sound of **laughter**. They think that this panting is the basis[3] for human expressions of **joy**— the 'ha-ha' sound we make when we laugh. When we find something **funny**, such as a **joke**, we laugh. When apes find something funny, such as a tickle, they laugh. Humans find many **situations** funny—such as jokes, tickles, TV comedy shows—but we are not **unique** because animals laugh, too.

[1]When you **tickle** someone, you touch them lightly with your fingers to make them laugh.
[2]When people or animals **pant**, they breathe very hard.
[3]The **basis** for something is the starting point from which it develops.

C | Write each word in blue from exercise **B** next to its definition below.

1. _____funny_____ (adj.) able to make one smile or laugh
2. _____unique_____ (adj.) the only one, one of a kind
3. _____Noise_____ (n.) a sound (often unpleasant)
4. _____researchers_____ (n.) people who study or investigate something scientifically
5. _____joy_____ (n.) great happiness
6. _____led_____ (v.) directed, showed the way
7. _____joke_____ (n.) a story that makes people laugh
8. _____recorded_____ (v.) made an audio or written copy of something
9. _____laughter_____ (n.) sounds of happiness or amusement
10. _____situations_____ (n.) the way things are at a certain time and place

A | Fill in each blank with a word in **blue** from exercise **A** on page 24. Use each word only once.

1. **A:** Social __situations__ such as parties sometimes make me nervous.

    B: Me too.

2. **A:** They felt great _____ when they held their first grandchild.

    B: I'm sure they were really happy.

3. **A:** So, who _____ the group discussion yesterday?

    B: Adriana did. She asked some really good questions about the topic.

4. **A:** There are several new _____ on Professor Watson's team.

    B: Interesting. What are they studying?

5. **A:** I like your new CD. The singer is very unusual.

    B: Yes, she has a _____ style.

6. **A:** Larry told a _____, but it wasn't _____. Nobody even smiled.

    B: Poor Larry!

7. **A:** I can hear _____ coming from next door.

    B: Yeah, they're watching their favorite TV sitcom[1].

8. **A:** I missed the lecture.

    B: Don't worry. I _____ the lecture on my computer. We can listen to it again later.

9. **A:** Your car is making a really odd _____.

    B: Really? Perhaps I should take it to a mechanic.

B | **Self-Reflection.** Form a group with two or three other students. Discuss the questions.

1. When was the last time you **laughed** a lot? What was **funny**?
2. What **situations** do you find **funny**? What makes you **laugh**?

> My children tell jokes. The jokes are so bad I laugh.

[1]**Sitcom** is short for situation comedy. A **sitcom** is a funny TV series.

Before Listening

👥 **A | Discussion.** Look at the photos. Then discuss the questions with a partner.

1. Both of these activities can be enjoyable. How are the people in the photos enjoying themselves?
2. Who in the photos is likely to laugh? Explain.

👥 **B | Predicting Content.** You are going to hear a lecture about laughter. With your partner, check (✔) the topics you think you will hear about.

❑ reasons people laugh   ❑ animal laughter
❑ examples of jokes   ❑ things that people are afraid of

Listening: A Lecture

Critical Thinking Focus: Understanding the Speaker's Purpose

When we listen to a lecture or a conversation, we need to know *why* the speaker is giving the talk, lecture, etc. This is the speaker's purpose. Sometimes speakers directly state their purpose, but often they do not. Listening to what speakers say and how they say it will help you understand their purpose.

Here are some examples.
The purpose of a political speech is often <u>to persuade or convince the audience to vote.</u>
The purpose of a TV sitcom is <u>to entertain the audience.</u>
The purpose of a college lecture is <u>to inform the audience.</u>

🎧 **A | Understanding the Speaker's Purpose.** Read the questions and answers. Then listen to the first part of the lecture and choose the correct answers.
track 1-17

1. What is the speaker's main purpose?
   a. to make us laugh   (b.) to give us information
2. Does the speaker directly state his purpose?
   a. yes   (b. no)

B | **Checking Predictions.** Look back at the predictions you made in exercise **B** on page 26. Then listen to the entire lecture. Which of your predictions were correct?

track 1-18

C | **Listening for Main Ideas.** Read the statements and answer choices below. Then listen again and choose the best word or phrase to complete each statement.

track 1-18

1. People usually laugh _____.
   a. at good jokes
   b. after they learn to talk
   c. when other people laugh
2. For rats, laughter is a form of _____.
   a. communication
   b. play
   c. research
3. People will probably *not* laugh _____.
   a. in a social situation
   b. when they're with friends
   c. when they're alone

commu

D | **Listening for Details.** Read the statements. Then listen again and complete each statement with information from the lecture.

track 1-18

1. Professor Panksepp, the rat researcher, works at _bowling_ State University.
2. The rats' laughter is at a very _high_ frequency, so people can't hear it.
3. More than _80 percent_ percent of laughter is *not* because of jokes.
4. TV comedy shows often use a _laugh_ track to make the audience laugh.

After Listening

Critical Thinking. Discuss the questions with a partner.

1. Do you think some people laugh more than others? If so, what do you think the reason is for this?
2. Is it always a good thing to laugh? Or, are there times when it is not good to laugh? Explain.

Language Function

Asking Questions to Show Interest

When we have a conversation, it is polite to show interest in what the other person is saying. Sometimes, we use an expression of interest followed by a question to find out more information.

A: *I don't like my new job.*
B: *Oh, why not?*

A: *The movie was just awful!*
B: *Oh, that's too bad. What didn't you like about it?*

A: *My vacation was fabulous. I'm so relaxed now.*
B: *Good for you. Do you have any photos?*

A: *It was a fascinating lecture.*
B: *Really? Why?*

A | Complete each conversation below with an appropriate expression from the box.

Good for you!	Really?	How funny!	Oh, that's too bad.	Oh, why?

1. **A:** I hate that new TV sitcom.
   B: *oh why ?*
   A: It wasn't funny!

2. **A:** Oh, I love this weather. It makes me happy.
   B: *Good for you* Most people don't like rain and cold.

3. **A:** I'm going shopping. I just got my paycheck.
   B: *Really?* Don't spend it all at once!

4. **A:** I'm studying to be a chef.
   B: *How funny* That's exactly what I want to do.

5. **A:** I didn't pass the test.
   B: *oh that's to bad* Better luck next time.

👥 **B** | Practice the conversations with a partner. Then switch roles and practice them again.

👥 **C** | Work with your partner and have a conversation. Student A: Ask Student B about what makes him or her laugh. Student B: Use the expressions of interest from exercise **A**. Then switch roles.

Grammar

The Simple Present Tense: *Yes/No* Questions

Yes/No questions are questions that we can answer with the words *yes* or *no*.

For *yes/no* questions with the verb *be*, we put *am, is,* or *are* before the subject.

Questions	**Answers**
Is the movie funny?	Yes, it is. OR No, it isn't.
Are researchers interesting people?	Yes, they are. OR No, they're not.

For *yes/no* questions with other verbs, we put *do* or *does* before the subject, and use the base form of the verb.

Questions	**Answers**
Do you **laugh** a lot?	Yes, I do. OR No, I don't.
Does he **tell** jokes all the time?	Yes, he does. OR No, he doesn't.
Do we **laugh** in lectures?	Yes, we do. OR No, we don't.

A | Complete the questions in the survey below. Use *do/does* or *are* and the verbs from the box.

have	do	like	have	keep

Survey: How Happy Are You?

1. __Are__ you a social person?   Yes   (No)
2. __Do__ you __do__ activities with other people?   (Yes)   No
3. __Do__ you __have__ fun with people?   (Yes)   No
4. __Do__ you __take__ a vacation every year?   (Yes)   No
5. __Are__ you middle-aged?   Yes   (No)
6. __Are__ you married?   Yes   (No)
7. __Do__ you __keep__ fit?   (Yes)   No
8. __Do__ you __like__ being outside?   (Yes)   No

B | Answer the questions in the survey. Circle *Yes* or *No*.

C | **Discussion.** Compare your answers from exercise **B** with a partner's.

Answer: If you answered Yes to all the questions, you are likely to be a very happy person!

Pronunciation

track 1-19

The Intonation of *Yes/No* Questions

Intonation is the rise and fall of your voice. When you ask a *yes/no* question, your voice rises or goes up on the last content word. Content words are *nouns, verbs, adjectives,* and *adverbs*.

Examples:

Do you think it is **funny**?   Is she really **laughing**?

track 1-20 **A** | Listen to and read these *yes/no* questions and answers. Underline the words where the voice rises.

1. **A:** Do you laugh a lot?
   B: Yes, I do.

2. **A:** Do you like weddings?
   B: I love weddings!

3. **A:** Do you like sitcoms?
   B: Some of them are OK.

4. **A:** Do you go to many parties?
   B: No, not really.

B | With a partner, practice the conversations from exercise **A**.

C | Take turns asking your partner *yes/no* questions about what he or she does to have fun.

| dance | go to parties | watch sitcoms | socialize with friends | play games |

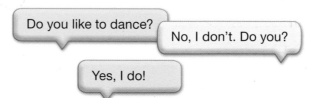

Do you like to dance?

No, I don't. Do you?

Yes, I do!

D | Form a group with two or three other students. One member of the group thinks of a well-known sitcom or movie. Other members of the group ask *yes/no* questions to find out what the name of the show or movie is.

Student A:	Is it a movie?
Student B:	No, it's a sitcom.
Student A:	Does this show come on at the same time every week?
Student B:	Yes, it does.
Student C:	Do older people like to watch this show?
Student B:	No, they don't.

Discussing Celebrations and Holidays

A | **Self-Reflection.** Think of a fun celebration or holiday. Read the questions. Then complete the chart with your answers.

	My Answers	My Partner's Answers
1. What's the name of the celebration or holiday?	Eid Yes	Eid they called
2. Do you celebrate it every year?	yes	of cours tow time's
3. Is this celebration in your home?	yes	yes it is,
4. Does your family get together?	Yes	yes, all of them
5. Do you eat a big meal together?	yes	what kind of food do you eat? meat
6. Do you sing or dance?	No	yes we have traditonal dance
7. Do you give gifts?	Yes	yes I do to my Parentse.
8. Is this a fun time for you? Explain.	Yes	yes it is, we have many things to do.

B | With a partner, ask and answer the questions from exercise **A**. Complete the chart with your partner's answers. Show interest and ask follow-up questions.

> Yes, we sing.

> Really? What songs do you sing?

C | Form a group with another pair of students. Report what you learned about your partner in exercise **B**.

A dragon float in a Chinese lunar new year procession, Singapore Island, Singapore

A family celebrating Thanksgiving together in Lincoln, Nebraska, USA

Nubían

Nubian women singing traditional songs at a bride's home

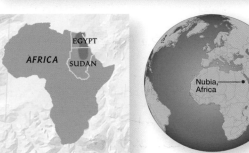

AFRICA   EGYPT   SUDAN

Nubia, Africa

Before Viewing

A | **Prior Knowledge.** In Lesson A you discussed holidays and celebrations. Check (✔) the celebrations you like. Discuss the reasons for your answers with a partner.

- ❏ a birthday
- ❏ a wedding
- ❏ a school graduation
- ☑ other _Eid_

B | **Understanding Maps.** Look at the map and fill in the answers.

1. The Nubian people live in ___north___ Africa.
2. The Nubian people live in parts of two countries:
   ___Egypt___ and ___Sudan___.

C | **Using a Dictionary.** Read about the Nubian wedding celebration you are going to see in the video. The celebration includes both Nubian and Muslim traditions. Use a dictionary to help you with the underlined words.

A Nubian Wedding

The music: At the beginning of the video, we see people from a <u>village</u> in Egypt. They are playing <u>drums</u>, singing <u>songs</u>, and dancing. It's all part of a wedding celebration.

The couple: The <u>groom</u>'s name is Sherrif. He met the <u>bride</u>, Abeer, two years before the wedding.

The food: In many cultures, a <u>feast</u> is part of a wedding celebration. In the video, the whole village eats a meal of rice and meat.

703-627

A man playing a drum

Women baking flat bread for a large wedding

O OZile   *Sami Khdera*

Wedding

D | With a partner, take turns asking and answering the questions about the Nubian wedding. Use the information from exercise **C** to answer the questions.

1. Where is the wedding? *a village in Egypt*
2. Who is getting married? *Sherrif and abeer*
3. How do the people at the wedding celebrate? *Play durm, dance*
4. What do the people eat at the wedding feast? *flat bread, rice and meat.*

While Viewing

A | Read the questions. Then write the answers while you watch the video.

1. How many days and nights is the wedding celebration?
   Seven days and seven night
2. Who comes to the wedding celebration? *hole village — 3*
3. Where do the people eat the feast? *in front in somebody house*
4. When do the bride and groom arrive at the party? *mid night*
5. What does the bride wear to the party? *nickless, white wedding dress*

Nubian women carrying wedding gifts for a bride and groom

B | Read the statements. Then watch the video again and circle **T** for *true* or **F** for *false*.

1. Life changed for the Nubian people in the 1950s.   T   (F)
2. The Nubians had to move because of the Aswan dam.   (T)   F
3. Mohammed Nour came here when he was 12 years old.   (T)   F
4. Nour thinks life is better now, in the new village.   T   (F)
5. Nour talks about the Nubian language.   (T)   F

After Viewing

Critical Thinking. Form a group with two or three other students and discuss the questions.

1. What surprised you about the video? Explain. *Still until noon. @ 7 days the wedding*
2. How is the Nubian wedding in the video similar to weddings in your country? How is it different?
3. What was the main purpose of the video?
   a. to tell us about life in a Nubian village
   b. to tell us about a Nubian wedding
   c. to tell us about Nubian history
4. In Lesson B, you will learn about how people use their free time to be happy. What do you do in your free time that makes you happy?

chef   chef

The hero

🎧 track 1-21 **A** | **Meaning from Context.** Read and listen to what four people say about their free time. Notice the words in blue. These are words you will hear and use in Lesson B.

I don't have much free time because I have a full-time job. I also have children, so I like to spend time with them. Sometimes we go to the beach, and sometimes we go to the park. For me, playing with my children has some important benefits: It makes me feel young and gives me great joy.

I enjoy taking walks in the park. I love being outdoors—seeing the trees and feeling the sun on my face. Basically, I'm always moving. Walking is good exercise. All that exercise keeps me healthy.

What do I do in my free time? Well, my hobby is cooking. It's a pretty common hobby, so I know a lot of other people who like to cook. Sometimes, my friends come over and we cook together. We laugh and tell stories.

When I want to relax, I listen to music at home. My favorite music is classical, especially Mozart. There's only one drawback to spending my free time at home: I almost never spend time outside.

Jordan

B | Match each word in blue from exercise **A** with its definition.

1. free time (n.) ___d___
2. benefits (n.) ___g___
3. enjoy (v.) ___e___
4. outdoors (adv.) ___b___
5. healthy (adj.) ___c___
6. common (adj.) ___j___
7. together (adv.) ___i___
8. exercise (n.) ___a___
9. relax (v.) ___f___
10. drawback (n.) ___h___

a. physical activity that keeps you fit
b. in the open air, outside a building
c. strong and well, not sick
d. a period when you are not working
e. to get pleasure or satisfaction from something
f. to spend time doing something calm and peaceful
g. advantages, good results of doing something
h. a disadvantage, something that can create a problem
i. with another person or people
j. usual, happening often

A | Read the article. Fill in each blank with a word in **blue** from exercise **A** on page 34.

An Urban Escape

In a big city such as Paris, people need places to live, shop, and work. Empty space can be hard to find. But the city government finds and keeps these empty spaces. People need places to spend their (1) _____, and parks are places that most people (2) _____.

The city of Paris spends a lot of money to create more parks and gardens. Some people think that the cost is a big (3) _____. So, why does the city do this? What are some of the (4) _____ of parks and other green spaces?

- **Better Health.** Having places to (5) _____ after work helps people feel good. Parks allow people to get (6) _____ such as walking and jogging. Being (7) _____ in the sunlight is good for people.

- **Better Environment.** Trees help to clean the air and make cities cooler. Clean air helps people stay (8) _____.

- **Less Crime.** Crime, such as robbery and murder, is (9) _____ in big cities. Research says that there is less crime in places with green areas around them.

- **Improved Education.** Parks are also a place for children to learn and play (10) _____. According to one study, children learn better after they play in a park.

A woman and her granddaughter spinning in the Jardin de Reuilly, Paris.

A woman reading on a bench in the Jardin du Luxembourg, Paris, France.

 B | **Critical Thinking.** Discuss the questions with a partner.

1. Why do people **enjoy** parks?
2. What are some **drawbacks** of spending money on parks?

Before Listening

Predicting Content. You are going to listen to a guest speaker talk about city parks. Look at the photo and discuss the question with a partner. What do you think the speaker will say about the relationship between parks, or green spaces and crime?

Central Park, Manhattan, New York City, USA

Listening: A Talk with Questions and Answers

track 1-22 **A | Listening for Main Ideas.** Read the statements. Then listen and complete each statement with the information you hear.

1. The speaker is there to talk about some of the _____ of public parks.

2. The speaker says that parks provide _____ benefits and social benefits.

3. The speaker says that _____ is lower in places with a lot of trees and green spaces.

4. The speaker says that healthy, happy people have fewer _____.

track 1-22 **B | Listening for Details.** Read the statements and answer choices. Then listen again and choose the correct answer.

1. The first question the speaker answers is about _____.
   a. the things families do together at parks
   b. the types of exercise people get at parks
   c. the number of people who go to parks

2. The second question the speaker answers is about _____.
   a. the health benefits of parks
   b. the education benefits of parks
   c. the environmental benefits of parks

3. The third question the speaker answers is about _____.
   a. the types of city parks
   b. the drawbacks of city parks
   c. the importance of city parks

After Listening

A | **Ranking Information.** In the Listening section you learned that city parks have several benefits. Rank the benefits of city parks 1 through 5 in order of importance (1 = most important; 5 = least important).

_____ People have a place to exercise.   _____ Cities are cleaner and cooler.

_____ Cities have less crime.   _____ People have a place to relax.

_____ Children learn better.

B | **Giving Opinions.** Work with a partner. Compare your answers from exercise **A**. Discuss the reasons for your decisions.

> I think the most important benefit is that cities have less crime.

> Really? I disagree. I think the most important benefit is that parks give children a place to play.

Pronunciation

The High Line is an elevated park on an old railway in New York City.

The Intonation of _Wh-_ Questions

In _wh-_ questions, the speaker's voice rises on the last content word and falls at the end of the question.

track 1-23

Where is the nearest **park**?

When are you **going**?

track 1-24

A | Read the two conversations. Mark the intonation you think you will hear in the _wh_-questions. Then listen and check your answers.

Conversation 1:
Candice: What's the name of the park?
Alexis: It's called the High Line.
Candice: Where is it?
Alexis: It's in New York City.
Candice: Why do people go there?
Alexis: It's a good place to relax.

Conversation 2:
Sam: What do you do in your free time?
Devon: I like to jog in the park.
Sam: Why do you do that?
Devon: It's good exercise, and I enjoy being outdoors.
Sam: When are you going next?
Devon: Tomorrow morning. Do you want to come?

B | With a partner, practice the conversations in exercise **A**. Then switch roles and practice them again.

Language Function

Making Small Talk

When people do not know each other well, they can be friendly by making small talk. One way to make small talk is to ask and answer questions about the weather and other topics.

Examples: *So, who goes to River Park?*
What's the temperature today?

 A | Read and listen to the conversation. <u>Underline</u> examples of small talk.

Shelli:	There are a lot of people here today.
Omar:	I'm sorry?
Shelli:	I said there are a lot of people at the park today.
Omar:	There sure are. It's a beautiful day to be outdoors.
Shelli:	It really is. What's the temperature today?
Omar:	I don't know, but it feels perfect. I'm here with my son.
Shelli:	Oh, which one is your son?
Omar:	That's him over there.
Shelli:	Really? He's playing with my son!
Omar:	That's your son? What's his name?
Shelli:	Robert, and my name is Shelli.
Omar:	Nice to meet you, Shelli. I'm Omar, and my son is Andy.
Shelli:	It's great that the kids can play here.
Omar:	It really is.

 B | Compare your answers from exercise **A** with a partner's. Then practice the conversation. Switch roles and practice it again.

Grammar

The Simple Present Tense: *Wh-* Questions

We use *wh-* words (*What, Where, When, How, Why, Who(m), and Which*) to ask for information.

> For *wh-* questions with the verb *be*, we put the *wh-* word before *am, is,* or *are*.
> ***What is** the name of your favorite park?*
> ***Where are** your parents?*

> For *wh-* questions with other verbs, we put the *wh-* word before *do* or *does*.
> ***When does** the next train **arrive**?*
> ***Who do** they usually **stay** with in Portugal?*

A | Complete the questions using the simple present tense.

1. When / you / get up <u> *When do you get up* </u> in the morning?
2. What / be _____ your favorite food?
3. Who / you / send _____ a lot of text messages or emails to?
4. How / you / relax _____ on the weekends?
5. Where / be _____ the closest park in this city?
6. Why / be _____ trees good for the environment?

B | With a partner, take turns asking and answering the questions from exercise **A**.

C | **Discussion.** Talk to your partner about one of the topics below. Your partner will listen and ask you questions. Then switch roles and discuss a new topic.

| a hobby | a favorite book or movie | a beautiful place | a family member |

> I want to tell you about my older brother.

> What's your brother's name?

D | Listen to the conversation. Then practice it with your partner.

track 1-26

A: Everyone's having a good time!

B: What did you say?

A: I said everyone's having a good time.

B: They sure are—it's a fun party!

Student to Student:
Asking for Repetition

Sometimes we don't hear part of a conversation. Here are some expressions you can use to let people know you didn't understand them.

Could you say that again?
What's that?
What did you say?
Could you repeat that, please?

E | Work with your partner and follow the instructions below.

Student A: Say the sentences below to your partner. When you see //////////, don't speak clearly.

Student B: Ask your partner for repetition when you don't understand something. Your partner will repeat the information using his or her own ideas.

Example: A: I heard that ////////// are on the exam.
B: Could you say that again? What are on the exam?
A: Verb tenses.
B: Oh, OK. Thanks.

A crowd at a foam party at a water park in Sudak, Russia

1. There's a free concert in the park on //////////.
2. The weather is beautiful today! It's //////////.
3. I like this class because //////////.
4. That's my friend over there. Her name is //////////.
5. The park is easy to find. It's next to the //////////.
6. My favorite way to enjoy nature is //////////.

You are going to give a short presentation about something that makes you feel good, such as a celebration, a holiday, or an activity you like to do in your free time.

A | Brainstorming. Write down some ideas for your presentation topic in your notebook.

B | Planning a Presentation. Choose one of your ideas from exercise **A**. In your notebook, write short notes to help you plan your presentation. Include ideas for your Introduction, Details, and your Conclusion. Use the example below to help you.

Topic: Chuseok in Korea

Introduction: Chuseok in Korea

                —important holiday; families get together; in autumn

                —eat special foods

Details: Food

                —feast for the whole family

                —always make songpyeon (rice cakes)

        Activities

                —some families go to cemetery to remember ancestors

                —my family remembers ancestors while we eat Chuseok foods

Conclusion: Chuseok celebrates family (living and dead)

        I love being with my family for Chuseok.

Presentation Skills: Speaking to a Group

When you are speaking to a group, you need to speak loudly enough for everyone to hear you. Try to speak clearly with good pronunciation. This will help your audience understand what you are saying.

C | Presentation. Form a group with two or three other students. Follow the steps below.

1. Decide who will present first, second, and so on.
2. While one person presents, the audience listens carefully.
3. After the presenter finishes, each person in the audience must ask one question—either a *yes/no* question or a *wh-* question.
4. The presenter answers each question.
5. Repeat steps 1 to 4 for each member of the group.

Treasures from the Past

Think and Discuss

1. What man-made objects do we find at the bottom of the ocean?
2. What can we learn about the past from these objects?

These coins and jewelry are from the Whydah Galley shipwreck.
The ship sank in 1717 near the coast of Massachusetts, USA.

Exploring the Theme:
Treasures from the Past

Look at the photos and read the captions. Then discuss the questions.

1. What kinds of man-made objects do you see on these pages? Where did people find them?
2. How do you think people used these objects in the past?
3. Why do people want to find these objects now?
4. Do you think it is important to try to find objects like these? Explain.

A diver explores the wreck of the ship *Liberty*, sunk by the Japanese in 1942, Bali, Indonesia.

Gold beads, chains, and **coins** found in a Spanish Armada shipwreck, Ireland

A diver discovered this **gold plate** by accident off the Florida Keys, Florida, USA.

A scuba diver examines a **bottle** found In the Aegean Sea off Serce Limani, Turkey.

A | **Using a Dictionary.** Listen and check (✔) the words you already know. Use a dictionary to help you with any new words. These are words you will hear and use in Lesson A.

track 1-27

❏ dishes (n.)	❏ find (v.)	❏ looked like (v.)	❏ objects (n.)	❏ ruled (v.)
❏ exhibit (n.)	❏ image (n.)	❏ nearby (adj.)	❏ recently (adv.)	❏ tools (n.)

B | Match each word with its definition.

1. tools _____   a. a short distance away, not far away
2. nearby _____   b. things used to make or repair things
3. recently _____   c. plates or bowls used to serve food
4. dishes _____   d. to locate, or to discover
5. find _____   e. not very long ago

C | **Meaning from Context.** Read and listen to the information. Notice the words in **blue**. Then write each word or phrase in **blue** next to its definition below.

track 1-28

An image of Cleopatra on an Egyptian coin

New Exhibit Opens Today

Queen Cleopatra VII **ruled** Egypt for fewer than 20 years. People are still very interested in her more than 2000 years later. But until recently, no one knew much about Cleopatra at all. We didn't even know what she **looked like** because there were no pictures of her.

Now, a new **exhibit** tells us more about Cleopatra's life. The exhibit has hundreds of **objects** such as jewelry, tools, and dishes. For the first time we can see Cleopatra's face! There are coins with Cleopatra's **image** on them.

1. _____ (n.) things you can see or touch
2. _____ (n.) a picture of someone or something
3. _____ (n.) a thing or group of things you can see in a museum
4. _____ (v.) governed or led a country
5. _____ (v.) had a similar appearance to another person or thing

Bas relief of Cleopatra with her son by Julius Caesar, Dendera, Egypt

A | Read the conversations. Fill in each blank with the correct form of a word from exercise **A** on page 44.

Devon: Where did Cleopatra VII live?

Brenda: She grew up in Alexandria and two
(1) _____ cities.

Devon: So, when did she become queen?

Brenda: She became queen in her teens, I think. Then, she
(2) _____ for nearly 20 years.

Alexandria, Egypt

Marc: What happened to Cleopatra?

Hitomi: Well, the Romans became the rulers of Egypt, and Cleopatra killed herself.

Marc: Wow, I didn't know that.

Hitomi: Then, after Cleopatra's death, the Romans destroyed anything with her (3) _____ on it— statues, pictures, coins, and so on. They didn't want the Egyptians to remember her. So, for a long time we didn't know what she (4) _____.

Kim: What happened to Alexandria?

Larry: Earthquakes[1] destroyed it. But (5) _____, archaeologists discovered parts of the city under the ocean.

Kim: Really? What did they (6) _____?

Larry: They discovered over 20,000 (7) _____, including beautiful (8) _____ for serving food and useful (9) _____ to help people do all kinds of jobs.

Boats above Cleopatra's lost city, Alexandria, Egypt

B | Work with a partner. Compare your answers from exercise **A**. Then practice the conversations.

C | **Discussion.** With your partner, discuss the questions below.

1. Talk about a person who **ruled** a country you know about. Where was the person from? What did he or she **look like**?
2. Think of an **object** that is very important to you. What is it? Why is it important?
3. What kinds of museum **exhibits** do you enjoy? Explain.
4. Do you like to visit historic places? Why, or why not?

[1]An **earthquake** is a sudden, violent movement of the earth's surface.

Pronunciation

The Simple Past Tense -*ed* Word Endings

For regular verbs in the simple past tense, add -*ed* to the base form of the verb (-*d* to verbs that already end in -*e*). Usually the -*ed* ending adds the sound /t/ or /d/ to the verb.

Examples:

track 1-29

look → look**ed**   live → live**d**   play → play**ed**
   My grandfather **looked** like his father.

If a verb ends in a /t/ or /d/ sound, the -*ed* ending adds a syllable. We pronounce this syllable /əd/.

Examples:

want → want**ed**   need → need**ed**   start → start**ed**
   They **decided** to make a map.

🎧 track 1-30 Listen and check (✔) the sound you hear for each word.

		/t/ or /d/	/əd/			/t/ or /d/	/əd/
1.	painted	❏	❏	5.	closed	❏	❏
2.	explored	❏	❏	6.	rested	❏	❏
3.	talked	❏	❏	7.	shouted	❏	❏
4.	divided	❏	❏	8.	watched	❏	❏

Before Listening

Understanding Visuals. You are going to listen to a talk about the lost city of Alexandria. Look at the map and read the statements below. Circle **T** for *true* or **F** for *false*.

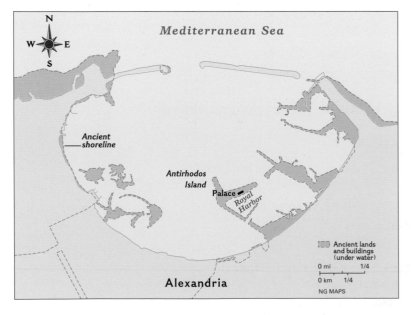

1. Ancient Alexandria is on land.   **T**   **F**
2. Cleopatra's palace was on an island.   **T**   **F**
3. Cleopatra's Royal Harbor[1] was to the north of Antirhodos Island.   **T**   **F**

[1]A **harbor** is a place on the coast that protects ships from the ocean.

Listening: A Talk about an Ancient City

Franck Goddio shows a bronze statue that was in the Temple of Isis.

 track 1-31 **A** | **Listening for Main Ideas.** Listen to part of the talk. Choose the best phrase to complete each sentence.

1. The ancient city of Alexandria _____.
    a. is only a legend
    b. was very rich and important
    c. disappeared 1000 years ago

2. Goddio's discoveries _____.
    a. give us new information about Cleopatra's world
    b. do not answer our most important questions about Cleopatra
    c. came too late to help historians today

3. Goddio knew that the underwater ruins[1] were _____.
    a. parts of the ship he was looking for
    b. ancient lost cities
    c. small enough to explore alone

track 1-32 **B** | **Note-Taking.** Listen to the entire talk. Complete the notes about Goddio.

Archaeologist Franck Goddio	Goddio's Team
• found cities that disappeared almost (1) _____ ago	• uncovered statues, (5) _____, musical instruments, (6) _____, and many other objects
• went to Egypt in (2) _____ to look for a sunken[2] ship	• made maps of (7) _____ Alexandria and two other cities
• found the (3) _____ of whole cities in the sand deep underwater	• explored Cleopatra's (8) _____
• started The European Institute of (4) _____ Archaeology	• found statues of (9) _____ and (10) _____ that were once in temples

track 1-32 **C** | **Making Inferences.** Listen again. Read the statements below and circle **T** for *true* or **F** for *false*. The answers are not in the speaker's exact words. You need to think about what you hear.

1. At first, Goddio did not know the importance of his discovery.   **T**   **F**
2. We still don't know what Cleopatra looked like.   **T**   **F**
3. It is taking a lot of time to study the ruins of the cities.   **T**   **F**

After Listening

Critical Thinking. Discuss the questions with a partner.

1. Do you think museums are important? Explain.
2. What can we learn by studying the past? Do you think it is useful or not? Explain.

[1]**Ruins** are the remaining parts of a destroyed building, town, etc.
[2]If something is **sunken**, it is under the ocean.

Grammar

The Simple Past Tense

We use the simple past tense to talk about completed actions in the past.

> It **rained** for three hours yesterday.   They **watched** a movie last night.

We add -ed to the base form of a regular verb to form the simple past tense.
We add -d if the verb already ends in -e.

> talk - talk**ed**   learn - learn**ed**   close - close**d**   like - like**d**

We need to make spelling changes when we add -ed or -d to some regular verbs.

> tr**y** - tr**ied**   carr**y** - carr**ied**   ro**b** - ro**bb**ed   sto**p** - sto**pp**ed

Many verbs are irregular in the simple past tense.

leave - left	eat - ate	go - went	read - read
find - found	give - gave	know - knew	quit - quit
fight - fought	come - came	take - took	meet - met

A | Fill in each blank with the simple past tense of the verb in parentheses.

1. The show _____*started*_____ (start) at 8:00 p.m.
2. My family _____ (live) in Taipei until 1998.
3. Linda _____ (move) to Buenos Aires when she (leave) _____ home.
4. Teodoro _____ (try) to call his parents last night.
5. That's a great book! I _____ (read) it in 2009.
6. Max and Ramona _____ (meet) in 1996.

B | With a partner, read the conversation and <u>underline</u> each verb in the simple past tense. Then decide how many syllables are in each verb. Look back at page 46 if you need help.

Sam:	Wow! I <u>learned</u> a lot from that class.
Coty:	Me too. I took a lot of notes.
Sam:	I heard a lot of noise from the hallway, though.
Coty:	I think the professor wanted to close the door, but it was too hot in the room.
Sam:	Yes. Oh, by the way, I finished my archaeology assignment.
Coty:	That's great! Were you at the library last night?
Sam:	No, I stopped going there to work. I don't like the library.
Coty:	Me neither. I studied in my room last night.

C | Practice the conversation in exercise **B** with your partner. Then switch roles and practice it again.

Language Function

A | Complete the conversations with *too* or *neither*.

Josie: You know, I really liked the exhibit.

Frank: Me (1) _____. Cleopatra was a very interesting person.

Josie: She really was. I didn't know she killed herself.

Frank: Me (2) _____.

Cho: Did you see the movie *Cleopatra* in Price Hall last night?

Jacqui: Um, no, I didn't.

Cho: Me (3) _____.

Lupe: I want to learn more about the *Titanic*.

Bruce: Me (4) _____!

 B | Work with a partner. Follow the instructions.

1. Choose one person to be Student A and one to be Student B.
2. Read your statements below and circle the word or phrase in **bold** that is correct for you.
3. Take turns saying your sentences to your partner. Your partner agrees with you by using *Me too* or *Me neither*.

Student A

1. I **like/dislike** historical museums.
2. I **got/didn't get** a lot of sleep last night.
3. I **like/don't like** the weather today.
4. I **studied/didn't study** a lot last night.

Student B

1. I **took/didn't take** the bus today.
2. I **like/dislike** chocolate ice cream.
3. I **got/didn't get** a lot of exercise last week.
4. I **like/don't like** learning about history.

Grammar

Yes/No Questions in the Simple Past Tense

We form *yes/no* questions with *be* by changing the order of the subject and verb.

Statements: *The Titanic **was** a big ship.*
*A lot of people **were** on the Titanic.*

Questions: ***Was** the Titanic a small ship?* *No, it **wasn't**.*
***Were** a lot of people on the Titanic?* *Yes, there **were**.*

We use the auxiliary *did* to form *yes/no* questions with other verbs.

Statements: *Bob Ballard found the Titanic in 1985.* *He **used** robots with cameras.*

Questions: ***Did** Bob Ballard **find** the Titanic in 1980?* *No, he **didn't**.*
***Did** he **use** robots with cameras?* *Yes, he **did**.*

Read the fact file below about the *Titanic*. With a partner, take turns asking and answering *yes/no* questions about the information. Use the words and phrases below.

1. the *Titanic* / leave Liverpool / April
2. the *Titanic* / arrive / New York / May
3. all the passengers / get into / lifeboats
4. the *Titanic* / sink / at night
5. Ballard / find / the *Titanic* / the Atlantic Ocean
6. Ballard / return / 1996

> Did the *Titanic* leave Liverpool in April?

> No, it didn't. It left Southampton.

The *Titanic*—Fact File

- April 10, 1912: The *Titanic* left Southampton, England. It never arrived in New York.

- April 14, 1912: The *Titanic* hit an iceberg[1] just before midnight.

- April 15, 1912: Some passengers got into small lifeboats, but there wasn't enough room for most of them.

- April 15, 1912: When the *Titanic* sank at 2:00 a.m., 1500 people were still on the ship.

In 1912, on its first trip across the Atlantic, the *Titanic* hit an iceberg and sank.

- August 31, 1985: Ocean explorer Bob Ballard found the *Titanic* on the bottom of the Atlantic Ocean. He used cameras and an underwater robot to see the ship.

- 1986: Ballard returned to the *Titanic*. He used a new robot to explore inside the ship.

Bob Ballard found the *Titanic* in 1985.

[1]An **iceberg** is a huge piece of ice floating in the ocean.

Talking about the Past

Understanding Visuals. Read the timeline about Bob Ballard.

The wreck of the *Titanic*

Childhood: Bob Ballard read books about shipwrecks[1] and dreamed of finding the *Titanic*.

July 1, 1985: Ballard and a team of scientists went to the area where the *Titanic* sank. They searched the area for several weeks.

August 31, 1985: Ballard's team found the *Titanic* in very deep water. They also saw many objects such as shoes and suitcases that once belonged to the passengers.

1986: Ballard returned to the *Titanic*. He sent a robot camera inside, and the team saw the grand staircase, the gym, and even the captain's bathtub.

2009: Two new research boats went into the water. Ballard designed them with the latest electronic equipment. Within hours, the boats started finding shipwrecks all over the world.

[1]A **shipwreck** is a ship that has been destroyed or damaged by an accident or storm.

Grammar

Wh- Questions in the Simple Past Tense

We form most *Wh-* questions in the simple past tense in the same way as *yes/no* questions, except we add a *Wh-* word, such as *why, where, when,* or *how* to the beginning of the question.

Was the Titanic *hard to find?*	**Why** *was the* Titanic *hard to find?*
Did the ship hit an iceberg?	**When** *did the ship hit an iceberg?*

Do not use *did* with *who, what,* and *which* when they talk about the subject.

✓ *Who discovered the* Titanic?	X *Who did discover the* Titanic?

Discussion. With a partner, discuss Bob Ballard's life. Use the timeline and your own ideas to ask and answer *Wh-* questions. Use *where, when, why,* or *how*.

> Why did Ballard look for the *Titanic*?

> As a child, he dreamed of finding it.

Treasures in Old San Juan

Fort San Felipe del Morro, Old San Juan, Puerto Rico

Puerto Rico, U.S.

The Capitol building, Old San Juan, Puerto Rico

Before Viewing

> The hospital is in a very old building.

> There are ancient coins at the museum.

A | Work with a partner. In Lesson A, you learned about some historical places and things. Make a list of three old or historical places or things in your city or town. Take turns talking about the historical places and things on your lists.

B | **Identifying the Simple Past Tense.** Read the information about Old San Juan, Puerto Rico, and underline the words in the simple past tense.

The Government Mansion, *La Fortaleza*

Old San Juan Quick Facts

- The Spanish explorer Ponce de Leon came to the island that is now Puerto Rico in 1508.

- San Juan became a city in 1521.

- There were huge stone walls around the city in the 16th century. A fortress[1] called *La Fortaleza* protected the city.

- Today, the governor of Puerto Rico lives in *La Fortaleza*.

[1]A **fortress** is a castle or other strong building that protects an area.

C | **Predicting Content.** Check (✔) the things you think you will see in the video.

❏ an airport ❏ new shopping centers ❏ a statue of Ponce de Leon ❏ tourists
❏ *La Fortaleza* ❏ old houses ❏ the ocean ❏ residents[2] of Old San Juan

[2]A **resident** is a person who lives in a place.

While Viewing

🖥 **A | Checking Predictions.** Watch the video. Check your predictions from exercise **C** in the Before Viewing section.

🖥 **B | Note-Taking.** Watch the video again. Write down three other things that interest you in the video.

1. _____ 2. _____ 3. _____

🖥 **C |** Watch the video again. Match each person in the video with the topic he talks about.

A street in Old San Juan

Person	Topic
1. Ricardo Rivera _____	a. the nice weather in Puerto Rico
2. Ricardo Alegría _____	b. the culture of Old San Juan: the music, artists, writers, and so on
3. Domingo Deleon _____	c. the way Old San Juan used to be in the 1950s

After Viewing

👥 **A | Discussion.** With a partner, discuss the questions below.

1. Why is the historical part of San Juan a good place to live?
2. Why is the historical part of San Juan a good place for tourists?
3. Which do you prefer for a vacation—historical cities or modern cities? Explain.

B | Using the Simple Past Tense. Read the information about Juan Ponce de Leon. Complete each sentence with the simple past tense of a verb from the box. Use each verb only once.

Colorful buildings in Old San Juan

go	give	fight	become	die

Juan Ponce de Leon

At the end of the 15ᵗʰ century, explorers from Spain and Portugal began arriving in the Americas. One of the explorers from Spain was Juan Ponce de Leon.

- He (1) _____ in the Spanish army before he came to the Americas.

- He (2) _____ the first governor of Puerto Rico.

- He (3) _____ the state of Florida its name. Florida is now part of the United States.

- Some people say he (4) _____ to Florida to look for the Fountain of Youth—a place with water that keeps people young forever. (The fountain has never been found.)

- He (5) _____ in 1521 after the Calusa Indians attacked him and his men in Florida.

A statue of Juan Ponce de Leon

🎧 track 1-33 **A | Using a Dictionary.** Listen and check (✔) the words you already know. Use a dictionary to help you with any new words. These are words you will hear and use in Lesson B.

❑ were made of (v.) ❑ everyday (adj.) ❑ route (n.) ❑ ship (n.) ❑ traded (v.)
❑ carry (v.) ❑ goods (n.) ❑ sailed (v.) ❑ silk (n.) ❑ valuable (adj.)

B | Understanding Maps. Look at the map and read the statements below. Circle **T** for *true* or **F** for *false*.

1. The ship sailed to China.   **T**   **F**
2. It took a route past Indonesia.   **T**   **F**
3. The ship went to the Middle East.   **T**   **F**

🎧 track 1-34 **C | Meaning from Context.** Read the article. Circle the correct word in **blue**. Then listen and check your answers.

The Shipwreck of an Arab *Dhow*

This is the story of an Arab (1) (**ship/sail**) called a *dhow*. The *dhow* left the Middle East, and it (2) (**traded/sailed**) east to China. There, the sailors bought (3) (**everyday/ valuable**) objects such as simple dishes, but also (4) (**valuable/everyday**) goods such as gold and (5) (**ship/silk**). Sadly, the ship sank near Belitung Island in Indonesia, and the sailors never returned home.

Travel was difficult in the ninth century, but not impossible. By land, there was the Silk Road. It was a way for people in one part of the world to (6) (**trade/carry**) with people in other parts of the world. By sea, there was the Maritime Silk (7) (**Route/goods**).

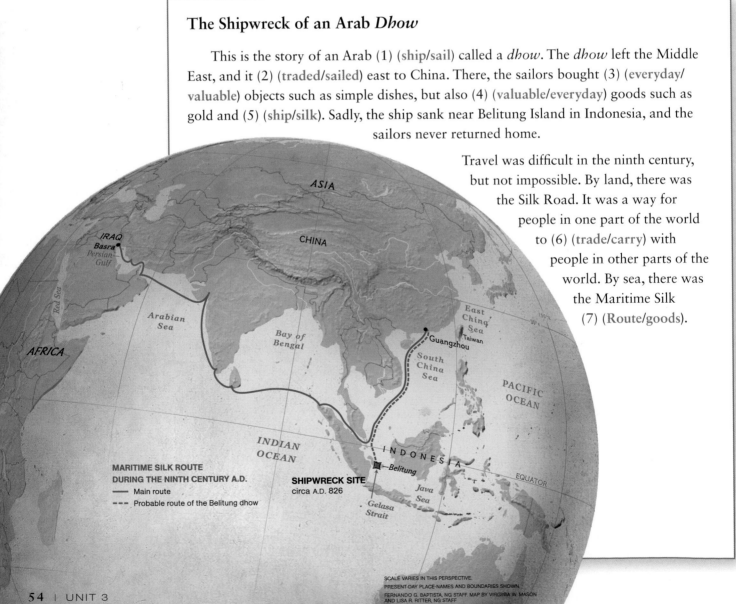

ASIA

IRAQ
Basra
Persian Gulf

CHINA

Red Sea

Arabian Sea

Bay of Bengal

East China Sea
Taiwan

Guangzhou

South China Sea

PACIFIC OCEAN

AFRICA

INDIAN OCEAN

I N D O N E S I A

EQUATOR

MARITIME SILK ROUTE
DURING THE NINTH CENTURY A.D.
— Main route
- - - Probable route of the Belitung dhow

SHIPWRECK SITE
circa A.D. 826

Belitung

Java Sea

Gelasa Strait

SCALE VARIES IN THIS PERSPECTIVE.
PRESENT-DAY PLACE-NAMES AND BOUNDARIES SHOWN.
FERNANDO G. BAPTISTA, NG STAFF. MAP BY VIRGINIA W. MASON
AND LISA R. RITTER, NG STAFF

A | Read the rest of the article. Fill in each blank with a word or phrase from exercise **A** on page 54. Then listen and check your answers.

track 1-35

More about the Belitung *Dhow*

A *dhow* was a type of ship that was common in the Indian Ocean and the Arabian Sea. *Dhows* were not very large, but they could (1) _____ a lot. Around the year 826, one *dhow* (2) _____ from the city of Al Basrah (now Basra, Iraq) to Guangzhou, China. There, the sailors (3) _____ with the local people, and they loaded the ship with the new (4) _____ they bought.

When the ship left China, it carried thousands of simple dishes and other (5) _____ objects. It also carried (6) _____ for making fine clothes, and a few very beautiful and (7) _____ objects. Some of these objects (8) _____ gold. (Recently, archaeologists studied the objects, and they think the gold objects were probably gifts for a royal wedding.)

The *dhow* chose an unusual (9) _____ home. Nobody is sure why the sailors took their (10) _____ so far south. Because of a storm, or perhaps an accident, the *dhow* sank between two Indonesian islands. Centuries later, in 1999, divers[1] found the dishes and other objects, as well as small pieces of the *dhow* itself.

The *dhow* carried 55,000 dishes that were made in China.

[1]A **diver** is a person who goes underwater, usually with special equipment.

B | **Discussion.** With a partner, discuss the questions below.

1. Which is more **valuable**, gold or silver? Explain.
2. In the ninth century, how long do you think it took to **sail** from the Middle East to China?
3. When did people find the Arab *dhow* shipwreck? How many years was it lost?
4. How do countries **trade** with each other today?
5. What **goods** does your country buy from other countries? What **goods** does your country sell to other countries?

3

A | Planning a Presentation. You are going to tell your classmates about your past. Check (✔) the ideas that are true for you. Write two more ideas about your past.

❑ I lived with my family.
❑ I learned to do something interesting (e.g., to play a musical instrument).
❑ I moved from one place to live in another place.
❑ I graduated from school.
❑ I got a job.
❑ I decided to do something important (e.g., to leave home).

Your idea: _____

Your idea: _____

Presentation Skills: Speaking from Notes

We often use notes when presenting to help us remember important points. It's important to make helpful notes and use them correctly. Here is some advice for making helpful presentation notes.

• Write your topics in the same order you plan to talk about them.
• Make simple notes that are large enough to read.
• Hold your notes down and keep them away from your face.
• Look down at your notes only when you really need to. Then look up and speak to your audience.

B | Organizing Ideas. Look at the student's notes below. Then make notes for your own presentation in your notebook. Use your ideas from exercise **A** and add interesting details about your past.

• My family lived in Pusan—12 years

• We moved to Seoul

• I learned to drive a car—18 years old—(funny story)

• I graduated last year

• I got my first job six months ago–in a bank

C | Presentation. Stand up and give your presentation for a small group.

D | Self-Reflection. Discuss the questions with a partner.

1. How well did you follow the advice about making and using your notes?
2. How helpful were your notes during the presentation?
3. How did you feel during your presentation?

Weather and Climate

Think and Discuss

1. Look at the photo and read the caption. When do you usually see this kind of weather?

2. Are you afraid of thunderstorms and lightning? Explain.

A bolt of lightning strikes the ground during a thunderstorm in Kansas City, Missouri, USA.

61

Exploring the Theme:
Weather and Climate

A | Look at the photos and read the captions. Then discuss the questions.

    1. What kinds of weather do you see on these pages?

    2. What is your favorite kind of weather? Explain.

B | Look at the information in the Extreme Weather chart. Then discuss the questions.

    1. Which place has the highest temperature? The lowest temperature?

    2. Which place usually has the most rain in one year? The least rain in one year?

Different Kinds of Weather

People shoveling snow after a snowstorm, **Colorado**, **USA**

Small, colorful boats tied up on a **sunny** day on Nusa Lembongan Island, **Bali**, **Indonesia**

People walking in Piazzo San Marco on a **rainy** day, **Venice**, **Italy**.

Palm trees on a **windy** day in **Florida**, **USA**

Extreme Weather

		Location	Date
Highest Temperature:	136°F (58°C)	El Azizia, Libya	September 13, 1922
Lowest Temperature:	−129°F (-89°C)	Vostok, Antarctica	July 21, 1983
Highest Annual Rainfall:	524 inches (1331 cm)	Lloro, Colombia	average over 29 years
Lowest Annual Rainfall:	0.03 inches (0.1 cm)	Arica, Chile	average over 59 years

Lightning and storm clouds over yellow canola fields, Calgary, Alberta, Canada

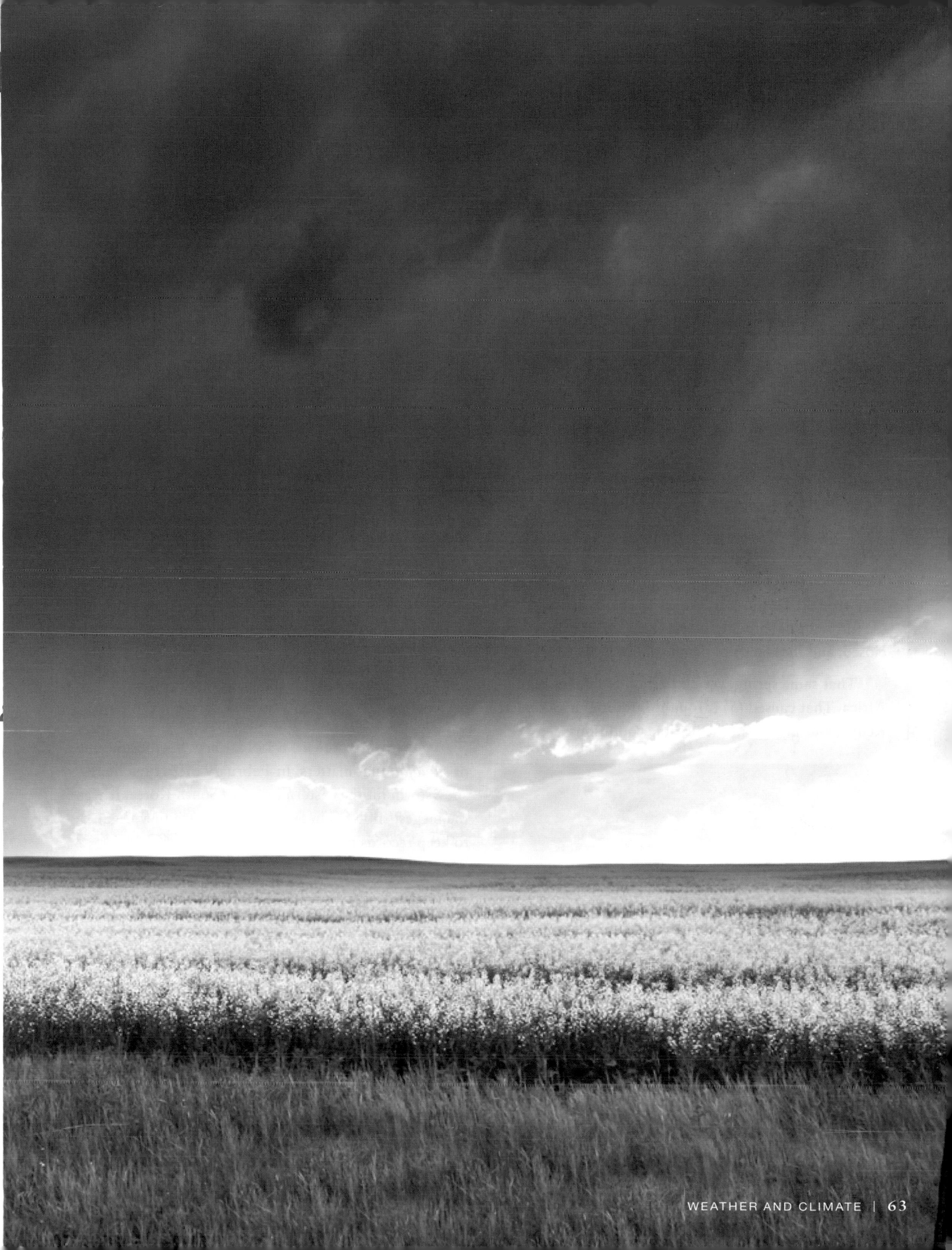

A | Note-Taking. Listen to a short conversation about global warming. Take notes about the effects of greenhouse gases.

track 1-45

 B | Understanding Visuals. Look at the diagram below. Use the words in the diagram, your notes from exercise **A**, and your own ideas to explain the process of global warming to a partner. Then switch roles.

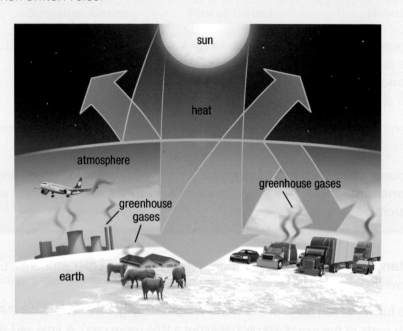

When we burn gasoline, oil, coal, and other fuels, greenhouse gases are the result.

C | Collaboration. With your partner, rank the ways people can reduce greenhouse gases in the air from 1 (most helpful) to 5 (least helpful).

_____ ride a bicycle or take the bus most places

_____ use less electricity at home

_____ plant more trees in cities

_____ buy local food instead of food from other countries

_____ recycle old bottles and cans

Presentation Skills: Making Eye Contact

Whether you are making a formal presentation or just speaking to the class, it is important to make eye contact. Eye contact lets your audience know you are talking to them, and it makes your audience *want* to listen to you.

If you are using notes, look up often and make eye contact. Each time you look up, look into the eyes of a different audience member.

 D | Form a group with another pair of students. Tell them how you ranked the items in exercise **C**. Explain your reasons. Practice making eye contact while you speak.

Focus on Food

ACADEMIC PATHWAYS

Lesson A: Listening to a Talk by an Anthropology Professor
Conducting a Survey

Lesson B: Listening to a Conversation between Students
Creating a Description with Interesting Details

Think and Discuss

1. What do you see in the photo?
2. What are some foods you eat almost every day?
3. What foods do you eat on holidays or on special occasions?

Farmers spread out apricots to dry in Anatolia, Turkey.

81

Exploring the Theme:
Focus on Food

Look at the photos and read the captions. Then discuss the questions.

1. What foods do you see in the photos?
2. Which of these foods do you like? Dislike? Explain.
3. Where are papayas from?
4. What are some foods that people typically eat every day in your country?

Foods from around the World

Cheese and other **dairy products** are popular in **Europe**.

African yams are a starchy vegetable.

Rice is part of many meals in **Asia**.

Many animals are raised for **meat** in **North America**. For example, cattle are raised for **beef**.

Papayas are a kind of fruit. They grow in **Central and South America**.

Australia and New Zealand are surrounded by water, so many people in these countries eat **seafood** such as **prawns**.

Bananas grow in the floodplains of the Nyabarongo River, Kigali, Rwanda.

LESSON A	BUILDING VOCABULARY

🎧
track 2-2
A | **Meaning from Context.** Look at the photos and read the captions. Then read and listen to the sentences below. Notice the words in **blue**. These are words you will hear and use in Lesson A.

The puffer fish can be dangerous to eat.

In some countries, people eat insects.

The durian has sharp spines on the outside and soft fruit on the inside.

1. The puffer fish is a poisonous fish, but the Japanese government will **allow** certain chefs to prepare it. They know how to make the fish safe to eat.
2. India is not the **only** country where people like hot foods. There are many other countries, too.
3. Insects are small but very **nutritious**. They are full of things that your body needs.
4. Many people can't **imagine** eating insects for dinner. It is a strange thing to think about.
5. I visited a rain forest in Colombia where the **local** people eat insects called termites.
6. Some people eat only **raw** foods. They think cooking food makes it less nutritious.
7. Many people eat honey. They like the sweet **taste** in their mouths.
8. Lingonberries are an **unusual** fruit. You find them in Sweden and just a few other places.
9. You can hurt yourself if you **touch** a durian fruit. You need to wear gloves to open it.
10. People in some parts of Asia think large water insects are **delicious**, so they eat a lot of them.

B | Write each word in **blue** from exercise **A** next to its definition.

1. allow _____ (v.) to let someone do something
2. raw _____ (adj.) uncooked
3. touch _____ (v.) to feel with your fingers
4. unusual _____ (adj.) not found very often, or interesting because it is different
5. only _____ (adj.) shows that no others exist or no others are present
6. delicious _____ (adj.) tasting very good
7. local _____ (adj.) belonging to the area where you live, or to the place you are talking about
8. imagin _____ (v.) to see something in your mind, not with your eyes
9. nutritious _____ (adj.) describes food that is good for your health
10. taste _____ (n.) the flavor of something, e.g., sweet or salty

USING VOCABULARY

A | Read the article. Fill in each blank with a word in **blue** from exercise **A** on page 84. Use each word only once.

Sharing Food and Making Friends

Dr. Wade Davis is an anthropologist. Anthropologists study people and cultures around the world. In each place he travels to, Dr. Davis likes to share meals with the (1) _local_ people. One food that made a big impression on him is the durian fruit. You might not have durian where you live. Southeast Asia is the (2) _only_ part of the world where it grows.

Sometimes it's hard to (3) _imagine_ why people eat the things they do. But everybody likes different things. In Malaysia, the durian is the "king of the fruits." Malaysians love it! They think it's (4) _delicious_. Some people say durian has a (5) _taste_ that's like vanilla ice cream with a little bit of onion.

The durian is a huge fruit—as big as a man's head. It's also heavy. You can only eat this fruit after it falls from the tree. But you can't just run up and (6) _touch_ it with your hands. A durian has sharp spines growing on it, and they can hurt you. Inside, though, the durian is soft. Some people like to cook it. Others prefer to eat it (7) _raw_. There's something else that's (8) _unusual_ about the durian. It has a very strong smell. Some people say it smells like dirty feet! Some people won't (9) _allow_ a durian inside their house.

People know that the durian is a healthy, (10) _nutritious_ food for the body. So people who don't really like the fruit hold their noses and eat it. For Dr. Davis, eating durian and other unusual foods shows respect for people and their customs. He also says that durian is good in pies!

B | **Self-Reflection.** Complete each sentence with your own ideas. Then share your ideas with a partner.

1. I think _pizza_ is **delicious**.
2. Sometimes I like the **taste** of _spice_, and sometimes I don't.
3. I can't **imagine** how people eat _such pork_.
4. I love to eat **raw** _fish_.
5. I think that _____ is/are **nutritious**.

Before Listening

 Prior Knowledge. You are going to listen to a professor talk about the importance of food in her work. The professor is also going to answer questions from students in the class. Discuss the following questions with a partner.

1. Do you feel comfortable asking questions in a small class? In a large class?
2. Do you think teachers want you to ask questions in class? Explain.
3. What do you think is the best way to ask a question in class? Circle your answer.

   ❏ Raise your hand and say nothing.
   ❏ Raise your hand and say the professor's name.
   ❏ Use a phrase such as *Could I ask a question*? or *I have a question*.
   ❏ Just ask your question when there is a quiet moment.

Listening: A Talk by an Anthropology Professor

track 2-3 **A** | **Listening for Main Ideas.** Read the statements and answer choices. Then listen to the talk and choose the correct answer.

1. The professor is _____.
   a. a biologist
   b. a psychologist
   c. an anthropologist

2. The professor showed the students _____.
   a. travel photos
   b. family photos
   c. interesting Web sites

3. The professor eats _____.
   a. anything except insects
   b. only foods from her home country
   c. everything the local people eat

track 2-3 **B** | Look back at the list in the Before Listening section. Then listen again. Check (✔) the ways you hear students ask questions.

Nopal cactus fields near Tlayacapan, Mexico

Prickly pear cactus leaves, *nopalitos*, ready for the grill in Yucatan, Mexico

C | Listening for Details. Listen again. Fill in each blank with the word or words that you hear.

1. For the professor, it's very important to become a part of the _____.
2. The professor eats unusual foods such as _____ ants.
3. *Cassava* is a kind of _____.
4. If it is raw, *cassava* can make people _____.
5. The professor never gets sick when she _____.
6. The professor likes to eat cactus with _____.

After Listening

 A | Self-Reflection. Form a group with two or three other students. Discuss the questions.

1. Do you like to try new foods? Why, or why not?
2. What non-nutritious foods do you like to eat? Explain.

 B | Critical Thinking. Discuss the questions with your group.

1. What foods from your culture might seem strange to other people? Explain.
2. What can we learn about people from the kind of foods they eat?

Cassava

Pronunciation

Can and Can't

In a sentence, the word *can* is usually unstressed. That means the vowel is reduced to schwa /ə/. The word *can't* is usually stressed and has a full vowel sound.

I **can** eat it, too.   I **can't** eat any kind of cheese.
You **can** use it to make bread.   You **can't** eat it raw.

There are two ways to hear the difference between *can* and *can't* in a sentence:

1. Listen for the final /t/ sound in *can't*.
2. Listen for the reduced vowel schwa /ə/ in *can*, and the full vowel /æ/ in *can't*.

In fast speech, we often don't hear the final /t/ sound, but the vowel sound can help you understand *can* and *can't* correctly.

With a partner, practice saying each pair of sentences. Use a reduced vowel for *can* and a full vowel (as in *cat* or *math*) for *can't*.

1. You can eat raw apples.   You can't eat raw *cassava*.
2. You can eat cactus raw or cooked.   You can't eat cactus with the spines.
3. I can help you tomorrow.   I can't help you on Sunday.
4. We can work on our homework together.   We can't work on the test together.

Language Function

> ### Expressing Opinions
>
>
> track 2-5
>
> In a conversation, we often use these expressions to show we are giving a personal opinion.
>
> ***In my opinion**, trying new foods is a lot of fun.*
> ***I think** the food in India is very good.*
> ***I don't think** durian fruit tastes very good.*
> ***For me,/To me**, this dish is too salty.*
> ***Personally**, I don't like the food at that restaurant.*

track 2-6

A | Listen to the conversations and <u>underline</u> the expressions for giving a personal opinion.

1. **Lydia:** I think these fried potatoes are delicious.

   Henri: I don't think they're good for you, though.

   Lydia: You're probably right.

   Henri: Personally, I don't like to eat any fried foods.

2. **Lee:** Do you like the chicken curry?[1]

   Zachary: In my opinion, it's a little too hot.

   Lee: Really? For me, it's perfect.

3. **Natalia:** What are you cooking? It smells great!

   Jenny: It's *falafel*. It's a vegetarian[2] dish.

   Natalia: Are you making any meat dishes to go with it?

   Jenny: Not tonight. Personally, I think we eat too much meat.

B | Practice the conversations in exercise **A** with a partner. Then switch roles and practice them again.

C | Work with your partner. Fill in each blank with a word or phrase from the Expressing Opinions box. Then practice the conversations.

1. **A:** _____ puffer fish is too dangerous for people to eat.

   B: _____ you're right.

2. **A:** _____ eating insects is a terrible idea.

   B: _____ I would like to try them.

3. **A:** _____ Frank is a very good chef.

   B: _____ he cooks eggs very well, however.

[1] **Curry** is a flavorful dish that is common in India and other parts of the world.
[2] A **vegetarian** dish has no meat in it.

Grammar

Can and Can't

We use *can* and *can't* to talk about <u>ability</u>.
> *I **can** ride a bicycle, but I **can't** drive a motorcycle. I don't know how.*

We use *can* and *can't* to talk about <u>possibility</u>.
> *You **can** write your paper about nutrition or about strange foods. You **can't** write it on any other topic.*

We use *can* and *can't* to ask for or give <u>permission</u>.
> ***Can** I come in? Yes, but you **can't** stay very long. I have to leave soon.*

The negative form of *can* is *cannot*. *Can't* is a contraction. It is usually used in spoken English.
> *Instructors **cannot** enter the building before 7:00 a.m.*
> *Could you speak up? I **can't** hear you very well.*

Note: In short answers with *can*, we use the full vowel sound.
> *Can you hear me?*   *Yes, I **can**. (/æ/)*

A | Fill in each blank with *can* or *can't*.

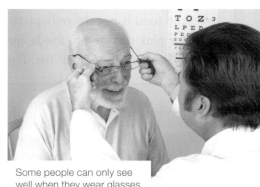

Some people can only see well when they wear glasses.

1. Lyle _____ pick you up at the airport. He'll be at work at that time.

2. You _____ use *cassava* like you use potatoes. It's delicious!

3. I'm sorry, you _____ go in there. They're having a meeting.

4. Students _____ meet with professors during their office hours.

5. Paula got new glasses, so she _____ see much better now.

6. I _____ eat this food. It's too hot for me.

B | Work with a partner. Take turns asking questions and giving short answers about the abilities below.

> Can you speak more than two languages?
>
> No, I can't.

speak more than two languages	play tennis well
cook Italian food	take beautiful photos
run very fast	eat very hot foods
play a musical instrument	name all seven continents

Situation: You and your group are restaurant managers. You plan to add three new items to your restaurant's menu. Research shows that people order menu items with good descriptions. You will create the best description for each new menu item shown on this page.

Form a group with two other students. Then follow the steps below.

1. **Discussion.** Look at the photos below and discuss some of the details about each new menu item. For example, does it contain vegetables, nuts, or tomato sauce? Will you serve it hot or cold? Use your own ideas.

2. **Brainstorming.** For each new menu item, make a list of several descriptive adjectives in your notebook. Look back at the chart on page 98. Use your dictionary to help you with other adjectives.

3. **Planning a Presentation.** Assign one menu item to each person in your group. Write notes for a description of your menu item. The words you choose should make people want to order the food.

4. **Presentation.** Describe your menu item to your group. Remember to use descriptive adjectives. Ask your group members if your description makes them want to order the item. Can they think of ways to make the description even better?

Fried vegetable egg rolls

Pasta with chicken and tomato sauce

Brownie with vanilla ice cream and chocolate sauce

Presentation Skills: Giving Interesting Details

Giving details keeps your audience interested and makes your presentation more complete. You can use descriptive adjectives and other expressions to add interesting details. For example:

Without Details: *There were flowers in front of the building.*

With Details: *There were fragrant red roses in large wooden flower boxes in front of Murphy Hall.*

Overview

The *Independent Student Handbook* is a resource that you can use at different points and in different ways during this course. You may want to read the entire handbook at the beginning of the class as an introduction to the skills and strategies you will develop and practice throughout the book. Reading it at the beginning will provide you with another tool to understand the material.

Use the *Independent Student Handbook* throughout the course in the following ways:

Additional Instruction: You can use the *Independent Student Handbook* to provide a little more instruction on a particular skill that you are practicing in the units. In addition to putting all the skills instruction in one place, the *Independent Student Handbook* includes additional suggestions and strategies. For example, if you find you're having trouble following academic lectures, you can refer to the Improving Your Listening Skills section to review signal phrases that help you to understand the speaker's flow of ideas.

Independent Work: You can use the *Independent Student Handbook* to help you when you are working on your own. For example, if you want to improve your vocabulary, you can follow some of the suggestions in the Building Your Vocabulary section.

Source of Specific Tools: A third way to use the *Independent Student Handbook* is as a source of specific tools such as outlines, graphic organizers, and checklists. For example, if you are preparing a presentation, you might want to use the Research Checklist as you research your topic. Then, you might want to complete the Presentation Outline to organize your information. Finally, you might want to use the Presentation Checklist to help you be a more effective speaker.

Table of Contents

Formal Listening Skills

Predicting

Speakers giving formal talks or lectures usually begin by introducing themselves and then introducing their topic. Listen carefully to the introduction of the topic, and try to anticipate what you will hear.

Strategies:

- Use visual information including titles on the board, on slides, or in a PowerPoint presentation.
- Think about what you already know about the topic.
- Ask questions that you think the speaker might answer.
- Listen for specific phrases.

Identifying the Topic:

Today, I'm going to talk about . . .
Our topic today is . . .
Let's look at . . .
Tonight we're talking about...

Understanding the Structure of the Presentation

An organized speaker will use certain expressions to alert you to the important information that will follow. Notice the signal words and phrases that tell you how the presentation is organized and the relationship between the main ideas.

Introduction

A good introduction should include a thesis statement, which identifies the topic and gives an idea of how the lecture or presentation will be organized.

Introduction (Topic + Organization):

I'll be talking about . . .	*My topic is . . .*
There are basically two groups . . .	*There are three reasons . . .*
Several factors contribute to this . . .	*There are five steps in this process . . .*

Body

In the body of the lecture, the speaker will usually expand upon the topic presented in the introduction. The speaker will use phrases that tell you the order of events or subtopics and their relationship to each other. For example, the speaker may discuss several examples or reasons.

Following the Flow of Ideas in the Body:

The first/next/final (point) is . . .	*First/next/finally, let's look at . . .*
Another reason is . . .	*However, . . .*
As a result, . . .	*For example, . . .*

Conclusion

In a conclusion, the speaker often summarizes what has already been said and may discuss what it means or make predictions or suggestions. For example, if a speaker is talking about an environmental problem, he or she may end by suggesting what might happen if we don't solve the problem, or he or she might add his or her own opinion. Sometimes speakers ask a question in the conclusion to get the audience to think more about the topic.

Restating/Concluding:

As you can see, . . .   *In conclusion, . . .*
In summary, . . .   *To sum up, . . .*
At the end, . . .

Listening for Main Ideas

It's important to tell the difference between a speaker's main ideas and the supporting details. In school, a professor often will test a student's understanding of the main ideas more than of specific details. Often a speaker has one main idea, just like a writer does, and several examples and details that support the main idea.

Strategies:

• Listen for a statement of a main idea at the end of the introduction.

• Listen for rhetorical questions, or questions that the speaker asks, and then for the answers. Often the answer is the statement of the main idea.

• Notice ideas that are repeated or rephrased.

Repetition/Rephrasing:

I'll say this again . . .   *So again, let me repeat . . .*
What you need to know is . . .   *The most important point is . . .*
Let me say it in another way . . .

Listening for Details (Examples)

A speaker will often provide examples that support a main idea. A good example can help you understand and remember the main idea better.

Strategies:

• Listen for specific phrases that introduce an example.

• Notice if an example comes after a general statement the speaker has given or is leading into a general statement.

• If there are several examples, decide if they all support the same idea or are different parts of the idea.

Giving Examples:

The first example is . . .   *Let me give you an example . . .*
Here's an example of what I mean . . .   *For example, . . .*
For instance, . . .   *. . . such as . . .*

Listening for Details (Reasons and Results)

Speakers often give reasons or list causes and/or effects to support their ideas.

Strategies:

- Notice nouns that might signal causes/reasons (e.g., *factors, influences, causes, reasons*) or effects/results (e.g., *effects, results, outcomes, consequences*).
- Notice verbs that might signal causes/reasons (e.g., *contribute to, affect, influence, determine, produce, result in*) or effects/results (often these are passive, e.g., *is affected by*).
- Listen for specific phrases that introduce reasons/causes and effects/results.

Giving Causes or Reasons:

The first reason is . . .   *This is due to . . .*
This is because . . .   *This is very important because . . .*

Giving Effects or Results:

As a result, . . .   *One consequence is . . .*
Consequently, . . .   *Therefore, . . .*
Another effect is . . .

Understanding Meaning from Context

Speakers may use words that are new to you, or you may not understand exactly what they've said. In these situations, you can guess at the meaning of a particular word or fill in the gaps of what you've understood by using the context or situation itself.

Strategies:

- Don't panic. You don't always understand every word of what a speaker says in your first language either.
- Use context clues to fill in the blanks. What did you understand just before or just after the missing part? What did the speaker probably say?
- Listen for words and phrases that signal a definition or explanation.

Giving Definitions:

. . . which means . . .   *In other words, . . .*
What that means is . . .   *Another way to say that is . . .*
Or . . .   *That is . . .*

Recognizing a Speaker's Bias

Speakers often have an opinion about the topic they are discussing. It's important for you to understand if they are objective or subjective about the topic. Being subjective means having a bias or a strong feeling about something. Objective speakers do not express an opinion.

Strategies:

- Notice words such as adjectives, adverbs, and modals that the speaker uses (e.g., *ideal, horribly, should, shouldn't*).
- Listen to the speaker's voice. Does he or she sound excited, happy, or bored?
- When presenting another point of view on the topic, is that other point of view given much less time and attention by the speaker?
- Listen for words that signal opinions.

Opinions:
I think . . .
In my opinion, . . .
Personally, I . . .

Making Inferences

Sometimes a speaker doesn't state information or opinions directly but instead, suggests them indirectly. When you draw a conclusion about something that is not directly stated, you make an inference. For example, if the speaker says he or she grew up in Spain, you might infer that he or she speaks Spanish. When you make inferences, you may be very sure about your conclusions, or you may be less sure. It's important to use information the speaker states directly to support your inferences.

Strategies:

- Note information that provides support for your inference. For example, you might note that the speaker lived in Spain.
- Note information that does not support your inference. For example, the speaker says she was born in Spain (maybe she speaks Spanish) but moved away when she was two (maybe she doesn't speak Spanish). Which evidence is stronger—the evidence for or against your inference?
- If you're less than certain about your inference, use words to soften your language such as modals, adverbs, and quantifiers.

She probably speaks Spanish, and she may also prefer Spanish food. Many people from Spain are familiar with bullfighting.

Summarizing or Condensing

When taking notes, you should write down only the most important ideas of the lecture. To take good notes quickly:

- Write down only the key words. You don't need complete sentences.

  ~~In~~ Okinawa, ~~people have~~ very low rates ~~of~~ cancer and heart disease compared to Americans. One ~~of the~~ reasons ~~for this is~~ Ikigai, ~~a Japanese word which translates to~~ "reason for living."

- Use abbreviations (short forms) and symbols when possible.

  info = information dr = doctor w/ = with < = less than/≠ fewer than > = more than

  b/c = because = /→ = leads to/causes 1/4 = one-fourth

Recognizing Organization

When you listen to a speaker, you practice the skill of noticing that speaker's organization. As you get in the habit of recognizing the organizational structure, you can use it to structure your notes in a similar way. Review the signal words and phrases from the Improving Your Listening Skills section.

Some basic organizational structures (and where they are often used):

- Narrative (often used in history or literature)
- Process (almost any field, but especially in the sciences)
- Cause and Effect (history, psychology, sociology)
- Classification (any field, including art, music, literature, sciences, history)
- Problem and Solution

Using Graphic Organizers

Graphic organizers can be very useful tools if you want to rewrite your notes. Once you've identified the speaker's organizational structure, you can choose the best graphic organizer to show the ideas. See the Resources section starting on page 214 in this handbook for more information.

Distinguishing between Relevant and Irrelevant Information

Remember that not everything a speaker says is important. A lecturer or presenter will usually signal important information you should take notes on.

This is important . . .   *Let me say again . . .*
The one thing you want to remember . . .   *Write this down . . .*

Instructors and other lecturers may also signal when to stop taking notes.

Signals to Stop Taking Notes:

You don't have to write all this down. . . .   *This information is in your book. . . .*
You can find this in your handout. . . .   *This won't be on your test. . . .*

In a similar way, they may let you know when they are going to discuss something off-topic.

Understanding Sidetracks:

That reminds me . . .   *By the way, . . .*
This is off the subject, but . . .   *As an aside, . . .*
On a different topic, . . .

Recognizing a Return to a Previous Topic

When a speaker makes a sidetrack and talks about something that is not directly related to the main topic, he or she will often signal a return to a previous topic.

Returning to a Previous Topic:

So, just to restate . . .
Back to . . .
Getting back to what we were saying . . .
To return to what we were talking about earlier . . .
OK, so to get back on topic . . .
To continue . . .

Using Notes Effectively

It's important to not only take good notes, but to use them in the most effective or helpful way.

Strategies:

- Go over your notes after class to review and to add information you might have forgotten to write down.
- Compare notes with a classmate or study group to make sure you have all the important information.
- Review your notes before the next class so you will understand and remember the new information better.

Independent Vocabulary Learning Tips

Keep a Vocabulary Journal

- If a new word is useful, write it in a special notebook. Also write a short definition (in English if possible) and the sentence or situation where you found the word (its context). Write a sentence that uses the word.
- Carry your vocabulary notebook with you at all times. Review the words whenever you have a free minute.
- Choose vocabulary words that will be useful to you. Some words are rarely used.

Experiment with New Vocabulary

- Think about new vocabulary in different ways. For example, look at all the words in your vocabulary journal, and make a list of only the verbs. Or list the words according to the number of syllables (one-syllable words, two-syllable words, and so on).
- Use new vocabulary to write a poem, a story, or an email message to a friend.
- Use an online dictionary to listen to the pronunciation of new words. If possible, make a list of words that rhyme. Brainstorm words that relate to a single topic that begin with the same sound (*student, study, school, skills, strategies, studious*).

Use New Words As Often As Possible

- You will not know a new vocabulary word after hearing or reading it once. You need to remember the word several times before it enters your long-term memory.
- The way you use an English word—in which situations and with what other words—might be different from a similar word in your first language. If you use your new vocabulary often, you're more likely to discover the correct way to use it.

Use Vocabulary Organizers

- Label pictures.

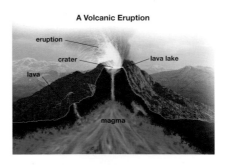

A Volcanic Eruption

- Make word maps.

- Make personal flashcards. Write the words you want to learn on one side. Write the definition and/or an example sentence on the other.

Prefixes and Suffixes

Use prefixes and suffixes to guess the meaning of unfamiliar words and to expand your vocabulary. Prefixes usually change the meaning of a word somewhat. Suffixes usually change the part of speech.

Prefix	Meaning	Example
a-	completely	awake
bi-	two	bilingual, bicycle
dis-	not, negation, removal	disappear, disease
pre-	before	preserve, predict
mis-	bad, badly, incorrectly	misunderstand, misjudge
re-	again	research
un-	not, the opposite of	unhappy, unusual

The following are derivational suffixes that change the part of speech of the base word.

Suffix	Meaning	Example
-able	adjective	available
-al	adjective	mental, controversial
-ary	noun	summary
-ent/-ant	adjective	different, significant
-ful	adjective	beautiful, successful
-ed	adjective	endangered, interested
-ical	adjective	logical, psychological
-ize	verb	summarize, memorize
-ment	noun	attachment
-tion	noun	information
-ous	adjective	dangerous

Dictionary Skills

The dictionary listing for a word usually provides the following helpful information:

Synonyms
A *synonym* is a word that means the same thing (e.g., *help—assist*). Use synonyms to expand your vocabulary.

Word Families
Word families are the words that have the same stem or base word but have different prefixes or suffixes.

Different Meanings of the Same Word
Many words have several meanings and several parts of speech. The example sentences for a word in a dictionary entry can help you figure out which meaning you need.

Collocations
Dictionary entries often provide *collocations*, or words that are often used with the target word.

Everyday Communication

Summary of Useful Phrases for Everyday Communication

It's important to practice speaking English every day with your teacher, your classmates, and anyone else you can find. This chart lists phrases you can use to perform each communication task—from more formal phrases to less formal.

Getting Clarification:
I'm not sure what you mean.
What did the professor mean by that?
Did you catch what the professor said about that?
Do you mean . . . ?
I don't understand.
Could you say that again . . . ?
What's that . . . ?

Expressing Thanks and Appreciation:
Thank you.
Thank you for . . . (e.g., doing something).
I appreciate it.
I really appreciate your . . . (e.g., help).
Thanks.

Agreeing:
That's true.
Absolutely.
I agree.
Definitely.
Right!

Showing Interest:
Oh, . . . ?
Oh, that's too bad.
Good for you.
Really?

Disagreeing:
I'm afraid I disagree.
That's a good point, but I don't agree.
I see what you mean, but I think that . . .
Are you sure about that?
I don't know . . .
Maybe . . .

Refusing:
Thank you, but (I have other plans/I'm busy tonight/I'd rather not/etc.).
I wish I could, but (I don't have a car/I have a class at that time/etc.).
I'm sorry, I can't.
Maybe some other time.

Inviting:
Would you like to study together this afternoon?
Do you have time before your next class?
Let's go to the art museum on Saturday.
What are you doing now?

Signal Words for the Future:
next (week/month/year)
in a (week/month/year)
after that
eventually

Showing Surprise:
That's unbelievable/incredible.
You're kidding!
Wow!
Really?
Seriously?

Congratulating:
That sounds great!
Congratulations!
I'm so happy for you.
Well done!
Good for you!
Way to go!

Making Suggestions:
I recommend/suggest . . .
Why don't I/you/we . . . ?
Let's . . .

Expressing Sympathy:
Oh, no, I'm sorry to hear that.
That's really too bad.

Making Suggestions (continued):	Asking for Repetition:
Maybe you could . . .	*I'm sorry?*
Why don't you . . . ?	*I didn't catch what you said.*
I recommend . . .	*I'm sorry, I missed that. What did you say?*
I suggest that you . . .	*Could you repeat that, please?*
Let's . . .	

Expressing Likes and Dislikes:	Asking Sensitive Questions:
I like . . .	*I hope this isn't too personal, but . . . ?*
I love . . .	*Do you mind if I ask . . . ?*
I can't stand . . .	*Would you mind telling me . . . ?*
I hate . . .	*Can I ask . . . ?*

Clarifying:	Interrupting:
What I mean is . . .	*Can/Could/May I stop you for a second?*
Let me explain . . .	*Can/Could/May I interrupt?*

Asking for Opinions:	Giving Opinions:
What do you think?	*I think . . .*
Do you agree?	*In my opinion . . .*
What's your opinion?	*For/To me . . .*
How about you?	*Personally, I . . .*

Doing Group Projects

You will often have to work with a group on activities and projects. It can be helpful to assign group members certain roles. These roles should change every time you do a new activity. Here is a description of some common roles.

Group Leader—Makes sure the assignment is done correctly and all group members participate. Ask questions: *What do you think? Does anyone have another idea?*

Secretary—Takes notes on the group's ideas (including a plan for sharing the work).

Manager—During the planning and practice phases, the manager makes sure the presentation can be given within the time limit. If possible, practice the presentation from beginning to end, and time it.

Expert—Understands the topic well; asks and answers audience questions after the presentation. Make a list of possible questions ahead of time to be prepared.

Coach—Reminds group members to perform their assigned roles in the group work.

Note that group members have one of these roles in addition to their contribution to the presentation content and delivery.

Classroom Presentation Skills

Library Research

If you can go to a public library or school library, start there. You don't have to read whole books. Parts of books, magazines, newspapers, and even videos are all possible sources of information. A librarian can help you find both print and online sources of information.

Online Research

The Internet is an easy source of a lot of information, but it has to be looked at carefully. Many Web sites are commercial and may have incomplete, inaccurate, or biased information.

Finding Reliable Sources

Strategies:

- Your sources of information need to be reliable. Think about the author and the publisher. Ask yourself, "What is their point of view? Can I trust this information?"
- Your sources need to be well respected. For example, an article from a journal of medical news will probably be more respected than an article from a popular magazine.
- Start with Web sites with *.edu* or *.org* endings. Those are usually educational or non-commercial Web sites. Many *.com* Web sites also have good information, for example www.nationalgeographic.com or www.britannica.com.

Finding Information that is Appropriate for Your Topic

- Look for up-to-date information, especially in fields that change often such as technology or business. For Internet sources, look for recent updates to the Web sites.
- Most of the time, you'll need to find more than one source of information. Find sources that are long enough to contain some good information, but not so long that you won't have time to read them.
- Think about the source's audience. If it's written for computer programmers, for example, you might not be able to understand it. If it's written for university students who need to buy a new computer, it's more likely to be understandable.

Speaking Clearly and Comprehensibly

It's important that your audience actually understands what you are saying for your presentation to be effective.

Strategies:

- Practice your presentation many times in front of at least one other person, and ask him or her for feedback.
- Make sure you know the correct pronunciation of every word—especially the ones you will say more than once. Look them up online, or ask your instructor for the correct pronunciation.
- Try to use thought groups. Keep these words together: long subjects, verbs and objects, clauses, prepositional phrases. Remember to pause slightly at all punctuation and between thought groups.
- Speak loudly enough so that everyone can hear.
- Stop occasionally to ask your audience if they can hear you and follow what you are saying.

Demonstrating Knowledge of Content

You should know more about your topic than you actually say in your presentation. Your audience may have questions, or you may need to explain something in more detail than you planned. Knowing a lot about your topic will allow you to present well and feel more confident.

Strategies:

- Practice, practice, practice.
- Don't read your notes.
- Say more than is on your visuals.
- Tell your audience what the visuals mean.

Phrases to Talk about Visuals:

This graph/diagram shows/explains . . .
The line/box represents . . .
The main point is that . . .
You can see . . .
From this we can see . . .

Engaging the Audience

Presenting is an important skill. If your audience isn't interested in what you have to say, then your message is lost.

Strategies:

- Introduce yourself.
- Make eye contact. Look around at different people in the audience.
- Use good posture. *Posture* means how you hold your body. When you speak in front of the class, you should stand up straight on both feet. Hold your hands together in front of your waist if you aren't holding notes. This shows that you are confident and well prepared.
- Pause to check understanding. When you present ideas, it's important to find out if your audience understands you. Look at the faces of people in the audience. Do they look confused? Use the expressions from the box below to check understanding.

Phrases to Check for Understanding:

Do you know what I mean?
Is that clear?
Does that make sense?
Do you have any questions?
Do you understand?

Understanding and Using Visuals: Graphic Organizers

T-Chart

Purpose: Compare or contrast two things, or list aspects of two things. We often write good things (pros/benefits) on one side and bad things or problems (cons/drawbacks) on the other. This can help people make choices.

Climate Change in Greenland

Benefits (good things)	Drawbacks (bad things)
1. _____	1. <u>Possible for oil to get into the ocean.</u>
2. _____	2. _____

Venn Diagram

Purpose: Show differences and similarities between two things, sometimes three. The outer sections show differences.

This information represents information that is true for both bear studies.

This area represents information that is true for the New Jersey Study.

New Jersey Study — *a bear's age*

Both Studies — *number of bears in the area*

Minnesota Study — *how cubs play together*

This area represents information that is true for the Minnesota Study.

Grids and Charts

Purpose: Organize information about several things. Grids and charts can show information in different groups, different time periods, different processes, or different qualities.

Noun	Verb	Adjective
exploration	explore	exploratory
	communicate	
	help	
		creative

Spider Map

Purpose: Help organize ideas for a presentation or writing assignment.

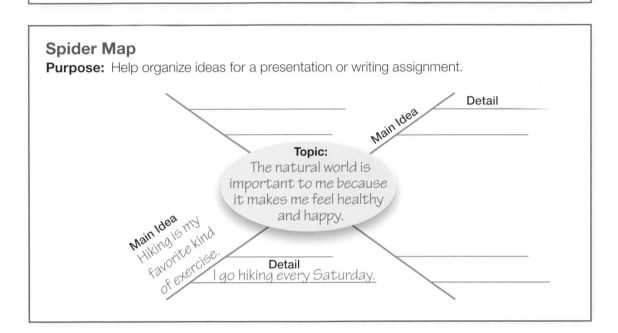

Detail

Main Idea

Topic:
The natural world is important to me because it makes me feel healthy and happy.

Main Idea
Hiking is my favorite kind of exercise.

Detail
I go hiking every Saturday.

Timeline

Purpose: Show the order of events and when they happened in time. Timelines start with the oldest point on the left. Timelines are frequently used to show important events in someone's life or in a larger historical context.

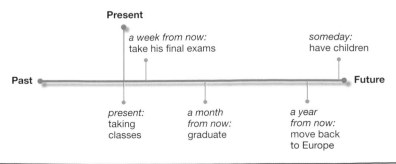

Present

a week from now:
take his final exams

someday:
have children

Past ●————————————————————● Future

present:
taking
classes

*a month
from now:*
graduate

*a year
from now:*
move back
to Europe

Reading Maps, Graphs, and Diagrams

Maps are used to show geographical information.

The **labels** on a map show important places mentioned in a reading or listening passage.

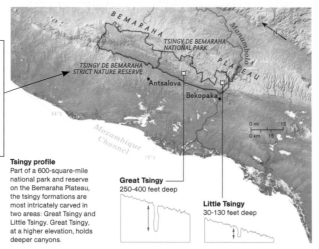

The **key** or **legend** explains specific information about the map. This legend shows the location of Madagascar and the Tsingy de Bemaraha National Park.

Tsingy profile
Part of a 600-square-mile national park and reserve on the Bemaraha Plateau, the tsingy formations are most intricately carved in two areas: Great Tsingy and Little Tsingy. Great Tsingy, at a higher elevation, holds deeper canyons.

Great Tsingy
250-400 feet deep

Little Tsingy
30-130 feet deep

Bar and **line graphs** use axes to show the relationship between two or more things.

Bar graphs compare amounts and numbers.

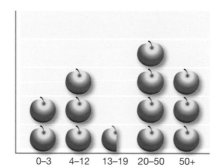

Daily Servings of Fruit

Age: 0–3 4–12 13–19 20–50 50+

Line graphs show a change over time.

The **y axis** shows the amount of sugar people eat in pounds

Sugar Use

(y axis: Pounds of Sugar, 0 to 160)
(x axis: Year, 1950 1960 1970 1980 1990 2000)

The **x axis** shows the year.

Pie charts show percents of a whole, or something that is made up of several parts.

This section shows that 26 percent of the people in Mexico work more than 48 hours a week.

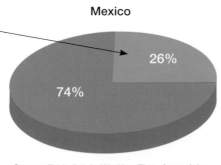

Mexico

26%
74%

Source: Table 3.4, in *Working Time Around the World* (ILO and Routledge 2007), pp. 46–51.

Diagrams are a helpful way to show how a process or system works.

The earth's atmosphere

Heat

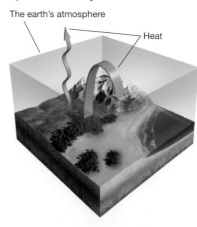

Presentation Outline

When you are planning a presentation, you may find it helpful to use an outline. If it is a group presentation, the outline can provide an easy way to divide the content. For example, someone could do the introduction, another student the first main idea in the body, and so on.

1. **Introduction**

    Topic: _____

    Hook/attention getter: _____

    Thesis statement: _____

    _____

2. **Body**

    First step/example/reason: _____

    Supporting details: _____

    _____

    _____

    Second step/example/reason: _____

    Supporting details: _____

    _____

    _____

    Third step/example/reason: _____

    Supporting details: _____

    _____

    _____

3. **Conclusion**

    Major points to summarize: _____

    _____

    Any implications/suggestions/predictions: _____

    _____

    Closing comment/summary: _____

    _____

Research Checklist

☐ Do I have three to five sources for information in general—and especially for information I'm using without a specific citation?

☐ Am I correctly citing information when it comes from just one or two sources?

☐ Have I noted all sources properly, including page numbers?

☐ When I am not citing a source directly, am I using adequate paraphrasing (a combination of synonyms, different word forms, and/or different grammatical structure)?

☐ Are my sources reliable?

Presentation Checklist

☐ Have I practiced several times?

☐ Did I get feedback from a peer?

☐ Have I timed the presentation?

☐ Do I introduce myself?

☐ Do I maintain eye contact?

☐ Do I explain my visuals?

☐ Do I pause sometimes and check for understanding?

☐ Do I use correct pronunciation?

☐ Am I using appropriate volume so that everyone can hear?

☐ Do I have good posture?

Pair and Group Work Checklist

☐ Do I make eye contact with others?

☐ Do I pay attention when someone else is talking?

☐ Do I make encouraging sounds or comments?

☐ Do I ask for clarification when I don't understand something?

☐ Do I check for understanding?

☐ Do I clarify what I mean?

☐ Do I express agreement and disagreement politely?

☐ Do I make suggestions when helpful?

☐ Do I participate as much as my classmates?

☐ Do I ask my classmates for their ideas?

Summary of Signal Phrases

Identifying the Topic:
Today, I'm going to talk about . . .
Our topic today is . . .
Let's look at . . .
Tonight we are going to talk about . . .

Introduction (Topic + Organization):
I'll be talking about . . .
My topic is . . .
There are basically two groups . . .
There are three reasons . . .
Several factors contribute to this . . .
There are five steps in this process . . .

Following the Flow of Ideas:
The first/next/final (point) is . . .
Another reason is . . .
However, . . .
As a result, . . .
For example, . . .

Restating/Concluding:
As you can see, . . .
In conclusion, . . .
In summary, . . .
To sum up, . . .

Repetition/Rephrasing:
I'll say this again . . .
So again, let me repeat . . .
What you need to know is . . .
The most important thing to know is . . .
Let me say it in another way . . .

Giving Examples:
The first example is . . .
Let me give you an example . . .
Here's an example of what I mean . . .

Giving Causes or Reasons:
The first reason is . . .
This is due to . . .
This is because . . .

Giving Effects or Results:
As a result, . . .
One consequence is . . .
Consequently, . . .
Therefore, . . .
Another effect is . . .

Giving Definitions:
. . . which means . . .
In other words, . . .
What that means is . . .
Another way to say that is . . .
Or . . .
That is . . .

Opinions:
I think . . .
In my opinion, . . .
Personally, I . . .
If you ask me . . .
I feel . . .

Signal to Stop Taking Notes:
You don't have to write all this down . . .
This information is in your book . . .
You can find this in your handout . . .
This won't be on your test . . .

Returning to a Previous Topic:
So, just to restate . . .
Back to . . .
Getting back to what we were saying . . .
To return to what we were talking about earlier . . .
OK, so to get back on topic . . .
To continue . . .

Understanding Sidetracks:
That reminds me . . .
By the way . . .
This is off the subject, but . . .
As an aside . . .
On a different topic . . .

Phrases to Check for Understanding:
Do you know what I mean?
Is that clear?
Does that make sense?
Do you have any questions?
Do you understand?

VOCABULARY INDEX

*These words are on the Academic Word List (AWL). The AWL is a list of the 570 highest-frequency academic word families that regularly appear in academic texts. The AWL was compiled by researcher Averil Coxhead based on her analysis of a 3.5 million word corpus (Coxhead, 2000).

ACADEMIC LITERACY SKILLS INDEX

Critical Thinking

analyzing information, 1, 2–3, 15, 18, 21, 22–23, 33, 35, 41, 42–43, 61, 62–63, 67, 72, 73, 75, 76, 81, 82–83, 87, 92

applying prior knowledge, 12, 32, 56, 66, 76, 86

assessing conversations, 97

brainstorming and, 40, 100

checking predictions, 27

describing foods, 99

determining interesting information, 91, 100

distinguishing between main ideas and details, 99

distinguishing between relevant and irrelevant information, 207

evaluating alternatives, 2–3, 10, 11, 13

evaluating the importance of the past, 47

explaining ideas and opinions, 2, 87

explaining reasons, 11, 13, 61

expressing ideas and opinions, 11, 37, 69, 90, 93, 95

identifying main ideas, 6–7

identifying what makes us laugh, 26, 27

making inferences, 7, 47, 57, 205

making lists, 71

meaning from context, 4, 14, 24, 34, 44, 54, 64, 74, 84, 94, 204

organizing ideas for a presentation, 60

organizing notes for a presentation
   chart for, 20

predicting content, 6, 36, 52

ranking items, 97

recalling facts, 59

recognizing return to previous topic, 207

recognizing speaker's bias, 205

reflecting on content, 6–7

self-reflection, 7, 17, 25, 31, 60, 65, 77, 85, 87, 97

summarizing, 206

understanding graphic/visual organizers
   charts, 4, 20, 31, 91, 95, 215
   diagrams, 80, 216
   grids, 215
   maps, 2–3, 32, 46, 54, 79, 216
   spider map, 215
   T-charts, 92, 214
   timelines, 51, 215
   Venn diagrams, 214

understanding speaker's purpose, 26

using new vocabulary, 5, 15, 25, 35, 45, 55, 65, 75, 85, 95

using notes effectively, 207

Grammar

a, an, any and some, 78

adverbs of frequency, 18–19

can and can't, 89

count and noncount nouns, 69–70

descriptive adjectives, 98–99

prefixes and suffixes, 209

verbs
   past tense signal words, 58
   simple past tense, 48
   simple present vs. present continuous, 9–10
   Wh- questions in simple past tense, 51
   Wh- questions in simple present tense, 38–39
   yes/no questions in simple past tense, 50
   yes/no questions in simple present tense, 29

Language Function. *See also* Grammar; Pronunciation; Speaking

adverbs of frequency, 19

agreeing, 210

asking for opinions, 211

asking for repetition, 39, 211

asking questions to show interest, 28

asking sensitive questions, 211

clarifying, 211

communicating that you don't understand, 8

comparing quantities or amounts, 79

congratulating, 210

disagreeing, 210

expressing agreement informally, 49

expressing likes and dislikes, 68, 211

expressing opinions, 88, 211

expressing sympathy, 210

expressing thanks and appreciation, 210

expressions of quantity with noncount nouns, 70

following the flow of ideas, 219

getting clarification, 210

giving causes or reasons, 219

giving definitions, 219

giving effects or results, 219

giving examples, 219

giving feedback while listening, 17

identifying the topic, 219

interrupting, 211

introducing topics, 219

introducing yourself, 20

inviting, 210

making informal suggestions, 57

making small talk, 38

making suggestions, 210–211

opinions, 219

phrases to check for understanding, 219

refusing, 210

repetition/rephrasing, 219

restating and concluding, 219